The EVENING

NEW YORK, TU

PRICE ONE CENT.

EXTRA

2 P.M.

SNOWED UP.

New York Still Held in the Blizzard's Grip.

Isolated by Snow From the Rest of the World.

Travel on Railroad and Horse Cars Stopped and Wires Down.

Extraordinary Experiences of the Past Twenty-four Hours.

The Worst Now Believed to Be Over—Hundreds Cross the East River on the Ice—New York Digging Itself Out and Walking Downtown—A Show of Operating the Elevated Roads—Downtown Hotels Crowded—Camping Out in Offices—Very Few Trips Made by the Ferryboats.

Having proved to its own satisfaction how it could paralyze New York if it tried real hard, the weather has consented to a cessation of hostilities and to give the city a chance to recover from the shock.

The snow stopped falling at 5.50 this morning, and at that time also the wind had subsided into something gentler and more to be sought for, though much less searching. The coldest part of the blizzard came last night and so did the darkest; for electric wires suffered with others of their kin, and gas mains were frosted out of all usefulness.

Reports from the South and from the At...

...office this morning, but reports from Chicago and the West came in as usual. It was...

ing at intervals of little l... half an hour. The c... at the Ba... end was and tra... filled ...inkling, the line... ple who ...'t get on ...hed far ...into the ...The au...ies pres... the same ...tions as ...esterda... allowed ... certain ...umb... assengers t... the sta...

...was closed ... were all ...rries s... it. Cath... rry was ...urthest ... of those ...g on the ...River.

WALKIN... THE E... ...m Fult... southw... eemingly ...ding to ...r's Isl... a sheet ...o so thic... olid that ...de a per...bridge ... York, ...t people ...cross ...ce struct... looked ...ly dari... ...with some a... safe passage, however, induced others to follow, and soon there was a black string of humanity stretching over the white field from ... to ... ore. Persons who didn't need to cross ... all walked over on the ice with the throng just that they might be able to tell of their experience.

The North River ferries were running under extreme difficulties.

SCENE ON THE RIVER.

An EVENING WORLD reporter, holding tightly to himself and his hat while walking in the stiff breeze over the roof of the Equitable Building this morning, saw in place of the river what looked like a ribbon of ice between New York and the Jersey shore. That it was not solid, though, was shown by the ferry-boats, tugs and craft which ploughed successfully, though laboriously, through it.

ON STATEN ISLAND.

Patrons of the Staten Island ferries, leaving New York hopefully last night, got to the St. George's landing, and most of them have been there ever since. The snow is as deep ... the houses ... are high and no trains are running.

Two boats made the trip from the island to New York yesterday morning, one in the af...

three unsu... attempt... passage Ca... ham orde... ...er to put back to ... City.

The same ... y was the ... perie... in making a ..., and the ... hat be done was ...up alongsi... an ...ing wharf a... the boat fr... e in night. The ... board did not m... for they h... in a supply ... liquor suffic... keep up the inn... th for an unli... period. The ... no ladies amon... assengers, and ... as it became e... that there was ... ting away for th... the young... ttled d... to ma... best of the ...

THE BRIDGE OF AN OCEAN STEAMER.

One of them produced a harmonicon, and for a time the crowd amused itself with music, the instrumentalist finally being drowned out by the voices of his companions, who became more and more noisy in proportion to the amount of liquid refreshment absorbed.

Several groups passed away the time playing cards, and at least two lively games of 25-cent limit were going on about midnight, at the same time that the wild carousing was going on in various other parts of the saloon.

There was very little sleeping done by any of the company, the principal reason being that the seats were not built that way. A few of the more weary made their beds on the floor of the cabin. The officers on board the vessel turned in early, and let the passengers do as they pleased.

The unhappy looking men that were landed from the Hudson City at Cortlandt street ferry about 7 o'clock this morning didn't spend much time waiting around. They had disappeared within five minutes after the gates were opened.

The ferryboats Chicago and New Jersey, also of the Pennsylvania road, were running at irregular intervals this morning. A great many people who got over to the other side of the river yesterday could not reach their homes in New Jersey, and were obliged to spend the night in the cars and the waiting rooms in Jersey City.

A large number of those people came back to New York early this morning for their...

SUPP...

Great Sc...

Something...

To add to th... by the blizzar... bilities ... ov... ...able... ...hey wer... ing upon the... from hand to t... coal or provisi... hours.

These peopl... retail dealers ... much valuabl... estimated ... dollars was ... yesterday thr... their places of... shops were no... pearance of ... worth while t...

And those w... to learn that t... sources of sup...

This is felt ... in the neigh... Washington M... but vegetable...

At Fulton M... are plenty, ... avail to him w... ing them.

Longshore... for delivering ... nearby consu... scenes in the ...

Early this m... Italians passe... carrying a qu... livering an o... to the Hotel ... hotels in Par...

The Astor ... this way a... taurant in P...

But Affairs ... downtown r... suspend busi...

At Mouqu... Open if the... enough...

...
Opposite ... his amou...

BLIZZARD!

THE STORM THAT CHANGED AMERICA

JIM MURPHY

SCHOLASTIC INC.

New York   Toronto   London   Auckland   Sydney
Mexico City   New Delhi   Hong Kong

ACKNOWLEDGMENTS

I want to acknowledge and thank the many individuals who helped me locate information and photographs for this book: Rebecca Streeter, New Jersey Historical Society; Nancy Finlay, Connecticut Historical Society; Barbara A. Brierley, Barnes Museum; Randy Goss, Delaware Public Archives; Roxanne M. Roy, Historical Society of Cheshire County, New Hampshire; B. Austen, Fairfield Historical Society, Connecticut; Anne Easterling and the staff of the Museum of the City of New York; Nicole Wells, the New-York Historical Society; and especially Arthur Cohen for his expert camera work and good cheer.

LIBRARY OF CONGRESS CATALOGING-IN-PUBLICATION DATA

Murphy, Jim, 1947–
Blizzard / by Jim Murphy   p. cm.
Includes bibliographical references and index.
Summary: Presents a history based on personal accounts and newspaper articles of the massive snowstorm that hit the Northeast in 1888, focusing on the events in New York City.

ISBN 0-590-67309-2

1. New York (N.Y.) — History — 1865–1898 Juvenile literature. 2. Blizzards — New York (State) — New York — History — 19th century Juvenile literature. [1. New York (N.Y.) — History — 1865–1898. F128.47.M96   2000
974.7'1041 — dc21 99-24894 CIP
10 9 8 7 6 5 4 3   01 02 03 04

Printed in the United States of America   24
First edition, November 2000
The text is set in 13-point Berkeley and the display type in CG Latin Elongated.
Book design by Marijka Kostiw

We gratefully acknowledge Joan Giurdanella for her meticulous fact-checking of the manuscript.

FOR CAROL AND JIM GORDON

GREAT NEIGHBORS AND FRIENDS WHO

APPRECIATE A GOOD SNOW JOB

WHEN THEY HEAR ONE.

TABLE OF CONTENTS

ONE • THE UNHOLY ONE   1

TWO • JUST A BABY   10

THREE • THE LAND IS AN OCEAN OF SNOW   25

FOUR • THIS IS ALL SO OVERWHELMING   41

FIVE • I WENT MAGNIFICENTLY ALONG   57

SIX • RULED BY WIND AND SNOW AND RUIN   71

SEVEN • WHAT WILL MY POOR CHILDREN DO?   84

EIGHT • IT IS ONLY A SNOWSTORM   103

NOTES ON SOURCES AND RELATED READING MATERIAL   125

INDEX   133

People out for a stroll in the city in early spring (AUTHOR'S COLLECTION)

O N E
THE UNHOLY ONE

On Saturday, March 10, 1888, the weather from Maine on down to Maryland was clear and unusually warm. A few scattered clouds scuttled across the blue sky, but little else marred what was a perfect day. Families went for picnics, took carriage rides, or strolled through their neighborhoods to see the purple and yellow crocuses bursting into bloom. The day was so nice that President Grover Cleveland and his wife left Washington, D.C., for a vacation weekend at their country home.

It had been one of the warmest winters on record in the East. This was especially true of the New York City area, which saw few frosts and little snow. Walt Whitman, the unofficial poet laureate of the *New York Herald*, was so taken by the endless string of balmy days that he penned "The First Dandelion" for Monday's early edition:

> *Simple and fresh and fair from winter's close emerging.*
> *As if no artifice of fashion, business, politics had ever been.*
> *Forth from its sunny nook of shelter'd grace —*
> *innocent, golden, calm as the dawn,*
> *The spring's first dandelion shows its trustful face.*

One of the few people unimpressed by the pleasant weather was John J. Meisinger, hardware buyer for the Manhattan department store of E. Ridley and Sons. On Friday, Meisinger had bought approximately 3,000 wooden snow shovels for $1,200. He had planned to keep them in the store's basement until the following winter. Unfortunately, a newspaper reporter heard about the purchase and wrote a satirical article entitled "Meisinger's Folly" that labeled him "Snow Shovel John." As he took delivery of his shovels that March Saturday, Meisinger discovered not only that he was the joke of New York City, but that his job was on the line as well.

Very few of the 15 million people living in the northeastern United States suspected that not one but two massive storm systems were heading their way. Reporter William Inglis certainly didn't as he boarded a pilot boat headed into the Atlantic; nor did seventeen-year-old Sara Wilson as she packed for her trip from Buffalo to New York City. Another seventeen-year-old, James Marshall, had no idea what lay in store for him; neither did former senator Roscoe Conkling, eighteen-year-old May Morrow, Long Island potato farmer Sam Randall, or cub reporter Richard C. Reilly of Brooklyn. Nine-year-old Gurdon Chapell and his four-year-old brother Legrand played happily on their Connecticut farm and never thought about the weather, while down in a small Delaware Bay town, divinity school student John H. Marshall (no relation to James Marshall) worked on the wording of his first sermon.

While all of these people went about their activities, one storm system was sweeping across Minnesota, Wisconsin, and Michigan, and dumping tons of snow along the way. If it held to its course, it would travel over most of New York and Pennsylvania before reaching the Atlantic. In the South, the second system moved over the warm waters of the Gulf of Mexico dragging along moisture-laden air. On that

Saturday, over four inches of rain deluged Pensacola, Florida, while cyclone-force winds tore up Tennessee, Alabama, and Mississippi.

All of this storm activity was being monitored closely at the U.S. Army Signal Corps in Washington, D.C. The Signal Corps was the precursor of our present-day United States National Weather Service and the agency charged with making weather "indications" (as forecasts were called at the time).

Three times a day, all 154 local weather stations telegraphed data about their regions to Washington, D.C., where it was carefully marked on maps and analyzed. The information included readings of the barometric pressure, temperature, humidity, wind velocity and direction, cloudiness, and precipitation. So complete was the information that the Signal Corps boasted it was correct 82 percent of the time.

After examining that day's data, the staff at the Signal Corps concluded there would be no real problem from either storm. The northern storm was losing strength, while the one to the south was on a path

On Saturday, March 10, the center of the northern snowstorm had nearly reached Lake Michigan, while the southern storm and its cyclone-force winds had crossed Arkansas and was about to enter Tennessee.

that would take it safely out to sea. The final indications for the following day were issued at 10 P.M. Saturday night: "Fresh to brisk winds, with rain, will prevail, followed on Monday by colder brisk westerly winds and fair weather throughout the Atlantic states. . . ."

At the New York City Weather Station, these indications and the accompanying data were read by staff member Sergeant Francis Long. Long was a big man, possessed of unlimited energy and an outgoing, friendly personality. He was also a minor celebrity at the weather sta-

tion for having survived three years of subzero temperatures and food shortages on an Arctic expedition.

Long glanced out his window at a clear, moonlit sky dotted with bright stars. The weather station was located at the top of the nine-story Equitable Building, then one of the tallest structures in the world.

Below him, the nighttime city sparkled and teemed with life — gas and electric lights, horse-drawn vehicles, steam-powered elevated trains, and scores of pedestrians on their way home from dinner, concerts, and

This view looking west across New York City was taken in 1894 from the World *newspaper building. Many of the buildings were designed to be massive and impressive, such as the Municipal Courthouse (LOWER RIGHT), while others seem to be reaching up to touch the sky. (NEW-YORK HISTORICAL SOCIETY)*

the theater. Many of these people were coming from a three-mile-long torchlight parade staged by the Barnum and Bailey Circus. Others headed up Fifth Avenue, where some of the country's wealthiest individuals had grand residences.

To the east, Long could see the wooden masts and rigging of forty or fifty sailing ships nestled around the five-year-old Brooklyn Bridge. The Great Bridge, as it was called, was not just the longest suspension bridge in the world; it was proof that science could overcome any earthly obsta-

This sumptuous living room shows how the very wealthy lived at the time. They often had recently refurbished rooms photographed, though usually without appearing in the scene themselves. (NEW-YORK HISTORICAL SOCIETY)

At the first sign of foul weather, many homeless individuals sought shelter in cheap flophouses. One rule of this establishment is PAYMENT IN ADVANCE. (AUTHOR'S COLLECTION)

cle. One commentator referred to it as a bridge to the future, calling it "a source of joy and inspiration to the artist, perhaps the most completely satisfying structure of any kind that [has] appeared in America."

In truth, New York City itself was considered a modern-day wonder. It was the financial and commercial hub of the United States, an emerging world center for art and architecture, the landing point of thousands of immigrants every day, and the place where the latest inventions — such as the telephone — were introduced to the public. French journalist Paul Bourget went to the top of the Equitable Building and was astonished by the city he beheld: "Seen from here it is so colossal, it encloses so formidable an accumulation of human effort, as to overpass the bounds of imagination."

On that Saturday night, of course, Sergeant Long's thoughts were much more practical. He scanned the sky for signs of trouble, then turned his attention to the work at hand.

Based on the Signal Corps's information, and supplemented by their own last-minute readings, the New York City Weather Station telegraphed its indication for the following day to area newspapers: "For Maine, New Hampshire, Vermont, Massachusetts, Rhode Island, Connecticut, eastern New York, eastern Pennsylvania, and New Jersey, fresh to brisk southerly winds, slightly warmer, fair weather, followed by rain. For the District of Columbia, Maryland, Delaware, and Virginia, fresh to brisk southeasterly winds, slightly warmer, threatening weather and rain."

That done, Long and the rest of the station's staff got ready to go home to observe the Sabbath. More data would be gathered before the official closing time of midnight, but essentially, their work was finished.

The same was happening at every other regional weather station and at the Signal Corps's headquarters in Washington, D.C. At midnight, the lights would be extinguished and the doors locked tight until 5 P.M. on Sunday afternoon. That meant that for seventeen hours there would be no one monitoring the changing weather patterns of the nation.

Long took the slow ride down to the street in the steam elevator, said good night to his supervisor, Chief Elias Dunn, and set off on foot for his home in rural Brooklyn. He was now just another citizen looking forward to his day off — and as unaware of the approaching monster as everyone he passed on the street.

For during the long hours while the nation's weather stations were idle, the weather underwent rapid and dramatic changes. The northern storm picked up energy over the Great Lakes region and continued its march east, bringing bitter cold and snow with it. The southern storm did, as predicted, wander out over the ocean. But instead of staying there, it turned during the night and headed north. As it moved along the coast, it gathered up more and more moisture and its winds gained velocity.

The two systems would eventually join into one massive storm. When people woke on Sunday morning, they were confronted by an ominously dark sky filled with fast-moving clouds and gusting winds. Many people had an unpleasant sense that some sort of living, and not very friendly, creature had arrived to menace them. Such feelings would color the way they thought and wrote about the storm for the rest of their lives.

A minister in a small New Jersey village looked up at the sky, then hurried indoors. "I had the strangest of feelings," he would tell his parishioners that day. "It was as if the unholy one himself was riding in those clouds."

T W O
JUST A BABY

On Sunday, March 11, young John Marshall took a stroll around the Delaware town of Lewes (pronounced *loo*-iss) with the pastor of the local Presbyterian church. Marshall's sermon had gone well that morning and he was happy about that. Still, the weather had changed drastically during the night, bringing cold rain and sharp winds.

At the beach, the water was choppy and restless, and the masts of anchored ships whipped back and forth, back and forth. Marshall's friend shrugged off the wind and rain as "just a bit of weather." Even so, Marshall thought he saw apprehension in the faces of the sailors as they peered up at the brooding, gray clouds.

And then there were the steamships, schooners, and tugs in the bay. Not one of them was headed out to sea; they were all hurrying into the safety of the Lewes breakwater. What did they know? Marshall wondered.

To the north and almost 20 miles from shore, twenty-six-year-old reporter William Inglis was seasick, groaning in his forecastle bunk and silently cursing himself. It had been his idea to write about the men who piloted ships into busy New York Harbor.

His editor at the New York *World* hadn't been enthusiastic about the idea at first, but Inglis had argued his case. The currents were treacherous in the lower harbor, he pointed out, and the heavy shipping traffic there required great navigational skill. These pilots did truly heroic work, he told his editor all too convincingly.

Inglis chose to go aboard Pilot Boat No. 13, the *Caldwell F. Colt*. The *Colt* was an 84-foot-long, two-masted schooner and one of the fastest and most aggressive boats in the New York Pilot Fleet. At the time, pilot boats would sail out a day before ships were expected and lay off Sandy Hook. The moment smoke was spotted on the horizon, all sails would be piled on and the pilot boats would race to the incoming vessel. Bigger ships paid higher fees, and the first one there got the job.

Eight other pilot boats were bobbing and rolling in the whitecapped water near the *Colt*, each carrying from four to six pilots. According to the shipping news, at least six large ocean liners were due in port at any

By the afternoon of Sunday, March 11, the center of the northern storm had entered Pennsylvania, bringing along freezing cold air and snow. Meanwhile, the southern storm had swung south toward the Gulf of Mexico, then begun moving north. In addition to extremely strong winds, this storm was also picking up great quantities of moisture from the Atlantic Ocean.

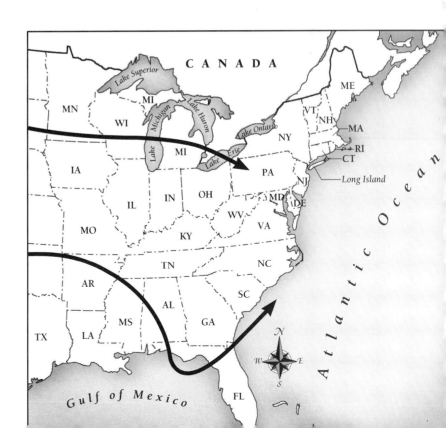

moment, along with from twenty-four to thirty-six freight-carrying vessels.

Despite the wind and a plunging barometer that promised an intense storm, the pilot boats stayed out, waiting and watching. This meant that Inglis had to wait, too, moaning in his bunk.

New York City on that morning was depressingly gloomy. The air felt heavy with moisture, and it was clear that rain would begin falling any minute. After hurrying to and from church, the majority of people settled in for a cozy day at home. Fires were lit, books and newspapers read, popular songs sung, and games were played and argued over.

Conversation was an important way to pass time in an era before the invention of the radio or television. One hot topic was the death of the ninety-year-old ruler of Prussia and Germany, Kaiser Wilhelm I, and the succession of his son, Kronprinz Friedrich, to the throne. The new emperor was himself extremely ill with throat cancer and many wondered how long he would live.

Sporting news from France also drew much comment. American bare-knuckle fighter John L. Sullivan had been held to a thirty-nine-round draw by Englishman Charlie Mitchell. This was surprising enough in itself, but most people were talking about the shocking things Sullivan's estranged wife was saying. "I wish Mitchell had killed him," Mrs. Sullivan told a *New York Herald* reporter. "He is a greatly overrated man. I hope he will die a beggar as he deserves to do for his ill-treatment of me."

Department store buyer John J. Meisenger was a hot topic that day, too, at least in New York City. Word of his snow-shovel purchase had spread, and one of the day's favorite bits of speculation was whether or not he would have a job come Monday morning.

Of course, the Signal Corps and all its local weather stations came in for verbal abuse as well. "I could have told them it was going to rain," scores of Civil War veterans announced loudly. "My leg hurt like it always does before a storm."

Others pulled out frayed copies of H. H. C. Dunwoody's 1883 bestselling book, *Weather Proverbs*, and proclaimed it the best way to predict the weather. The more pious reached for their family Bibles when the subject of predicting the weather came up, and quoted Job 37:16: "Can any understand the spreadings of the clouds?"

Naturally, some people did venture out. No matter how threatening the weather, there are always those restless, bored, foolish, or curious enough to chance fate. Families went for scheduled visits, and kids played in the courtyards, alleys, and streets near their homes — at least until a hard, cold rain drove them indoors in the afternoon.

Almost all restaurants, theaters, shops, concert halls, and other commercial businesses were shut tight on Sunday, the result of strict Sabbath laws. New York City's reform mayor, Abram Hewitt, had managed to get special licenses for a limited number of cafes, clubs, and music halls, and these places were jammed that night. Also busy were the many illegal beer halls and slop houses, where food and drink were inexpensive and a stove might give off some heat.

A day like this was always hardest on the poor. Those in unheated rooms either put on several layers of clothing to fight off the damp chill, or they stayed in bed. With few people wandering about, beggars had little chance to get the nickels and pennies necessary to buy a meal. Homeless children sought refuge in the hallways and cellars of tenement buildings, while hungry adults lined up at private charity shelters for soup and bread.

As the day progressed, the rain became heavier and the wind more fierce. By 3 P.M. Sunday, the giant storm system stretched from Canada down to Virginia, with the front cutting right through the middle of Pennsylvania. The front continued to move east until it reached the coast, where it slowed to a near stop, held in position by a mass of freezing Canadian air.

The center of the storm hung off the coast of Virginia at 10 P.M. Around this center, winds moved in a counterclockwise direction, which sent a cold gale out over the Atlantic, where it gathered up moisture. The mix of frigid air and warm water caused the moisture to condense and fall as either an icy rain or snow. At the same time, hurricane-force winds developed.

The change on the ground was sudden and dramatic. Heavy rains deluged Norfolk, Virginia, and Philadelphia. The same intense rain hit New York City, but here the temperatures had dropped to the freezing point. The wind-blown rain quickly covered streets, sidewalks, buildings, elevated railroad tracks, and lampposts with a dangerously slippery coat of ice. In the New England states, temperatures plummeted between 10 and 20 degrees in an hour, and moisture fell as snow whipped about by savage gusts of wind.

It all happened so suddenly that many of those who had ventured out earlier in the day found themselves trapped in a wild storm. James Algeo, his wife, and four-year-old son

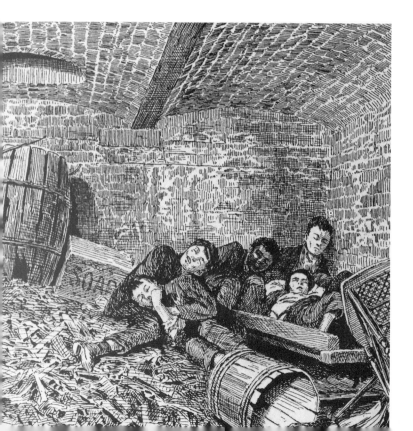

When the rains began to fall, these homeless boys had nowhere to go but to this coal cellar under the sidewalk. (AUTHOR'S COLLECTION)

As the storm begins, a wealthy man and his wife try to ignore a poor family warming themselves over a steam grate. (AUTHOR'S COLLECTION)

were in the Bronx visiting friends when the weather changed. Even though a heavy rain was falling at 8 P.M., they left for home anyway.

A thick buildup of ice made the streetcar jump the tracks several times, while slippery rails forced the elevated train to crawl along. The worst part of the Algeos' journey was the two-block walk from the station on 86th Street to their front door. A vicious wind-driven sleet slashed at their faces, numbed their fingers, and caused them to slip and slide all over the icy sidewalk. The trip to the Bronx had taken one hour; the return journey was a hard four-hour trek. When they stumbled inside at midnight, James remembered that a fine snow had just begun to fall.

Despite the severe storm, many people still had work to perform. Train engineers and conductors, the operators of horse-drawn cars, doctors making house calls, telegraph operators, ministers, priests and rabbis, bridge operators, police and firefighters — in short, the thousands of individuals who kept the cities and towns safe and running smoothly — had to brave the storm.

At the time, farmers still made up the single largest group of workers in the United States. Even though factory and office jobs were drawing an increasing number of people to urban areas, over half of the nation's population lived in the country.

Out on Long Island, for instance, seventy-year-old potato farmer Sam Randall had left his plow in the barn that day and stayed indoors whenever possible. But Sam had several cows, plus his plow horses and chickens, to feed and water. Three times that Sunday, he bundled up and hurried through the icy rain to the barn where his animals were sheltered. It was only 150 feet from his back door to the barn, but he was soaked through to the skin by the time he got inside.

The men at the New York City Weather Station had work to do, too. Chief Elias Dunn, Sergeant Francis Long, and the rest of the staff dutifully arrived at the Equitable Building at 5 P.M. sharp on Sunday and began collecting fresh data. The team was instantly aware that something calamitous was in progress: All telegraph contact with Washington was dead. What was going on down there? they wondered.

William Inglis could have given them some idea about what was happening — and what was on the way. Throughout the morning and early afternoon, the pilot-boat captains had watched the storm moving closer. Then, suddenly, the wind shifted to the northwest, wind velocity increased, the temperature dropped, and a blinding snow enveloped them.

The *Colt* now bounced and swung about on the roiling ocean, with captain and crew battling to keep it from rolling over and flooding. To his painful moaning, William Inglis added a new activity — praying.

It wasn't just ships far out at sea that were getting pounded. Down in Lewes, John Marshall was woken from a deep and peaceful sleep by shouting on the road below his window. "To the pier," voices were calling out in the dark. "Hurry! To the pier!"

Marshall glanced out his window. Through a thick, wet snow he could make out the shapes of men running frantically along Kings Highway toward the beach. He dressed quickly and dashed after the slicker-clad figures, barely able to keep his footing on the icy road.

Once at the pier, he saw immediately what had happened. The sudden, violent shift of wind had caught thirty-five ships in the breakwater by complete surprise. Tall masts had snapped like matchsticks and heavy anchor chains strained under the pressure of the thrashing ships, then broke. Before the crews could respond, steamships, schooners, and tugs were bobbing freely and smashing into one another like toys in a child's bath.

As Marshall and 200 others on shore watched, a tug hit the pier and sliced right through the massive timbers. The heavy surf then picked up the boat and tossed it onto the beach. A second tug hit the pier in another spot. This tug's captain managed to get his engines going, but as he backed away, he struck the steamship *Tamesei* and both vessels began to sink.

Some *Tamesei* crewmen leaped to a small portion of the pier nearby. This was the outermost part of the pier, 1,500 feet from land, and on the verge of collapse. But to the men of the *Tamesei*, it was better than being on a sinking piece of metal.

Meanwhile, the tug *Protector* saw what had happened and valiantly

The beach at Lewes is littered with debris from ships, while a two-masted schooner wallows in shallow water. The Lewes Lifesaving Station is in the center left of the photo. (DELAWARE PUBLIC ARCHIVES)

chugged in to rescue those on the sinking tug. Most of the tug's crew (and this included the captain's wife) were able to leap to the safety of the *Protector's* deck. Then, as the tug went under, a wave swept the mate and one crewman into the water. Luck was with them. The churning waves carried them along until they were close enough to the pier to be pulled to safety by those already there. Another vessel would ram the pier later in the night, and some of its crew would also find refuge on the shaky pier pilings, bringing the number of outcasts there to eleven.

From the distant shore, this drama was nothing but a series of murky silhouettes, accented by the thudding boom of ships crashing into one another and the distant, plaintive cries of the men for help. Rescuers could do nothing for them. A boat would have to be sent to save them, but with the waves running 15 feet high, this was a job for the professional lifesavers and their self-bailing surfboat. Unfortunately, the crew from Lewes was miles away, rescuing survivors from the seventeen schooners and freighters that had already gone aground.

John Marshall and everyone else did what they could, hauling scores of seamen from the frothing water and aiding the injured. Eventually, the men from the Lewes Lifesaving Station arrived and commenced their work. In all, the lifesavers rescued forty people at the Lewes breakwater, including all eleven men frozen to the pilings. Twenty-two men fell into the churning waters and were lost.

John Marshall wasn't able to witness the final rescues. His clothes soaked through, his face raw and cut from the flying sand, the young man made his way back to his host's home to change and pack. He had witnessed the awesome power of nature firsthand and seen how helpless humans were in the face of the storm's wrath. He'd also observed courage and bravery beyond description, and, yes, miracles. There was no doubt that God's hand had played a part in the rescues, but he had to wonder to what purpose God had sent the awful storm in the first place.

With these thoughts in mind, John Marshall boarded a train bound for Princeton, along with four other passengers. The train chugged ahead for a few miles, then came to a bone-jarring halt. The winds had pushed a giant wall of snow over the tracks, and the train had rammed it so hard that every car was completely covered. Marshall found himself trapped, much like the helpless seamen had been trapped on the pier, in a snowbound prison.

Over 400 miles away from Lewes, another drama was unfolding. The New York *Flyer* carrying seventeen-year-old Sara Wilson left Buffalo at precisely 5 P.M. On time, of course. The sky to the south was dark and threatening, but the conductor was confident that they would reach

New York's Grand Central Depot at the scheduled time of 7:30 A.M. Monday. Sara settled back into the big, comfortable passenger chair and opened her book.

She may have appeared calm and relaxed to others in the car, but Sara was really a bundle of emotions — nervous and excited, eager and apprehensive. This was her first trip on a train and her first time away from home on her own.

Less than an hour after leaving Buffalo, rain began splattering against the windows. The cars were buffeted by strong winds, and passengers could see the passing trees being whipped back and forth in a wild dance. When the rain increased to a downpour, talk in the parlor car took on an uneasy edge. Still, the conductor was able to announce with confidence that the train was running on schedule.

Sara tried to read, but the swaying of the car and fatigue won out, and she was soon asleep. Hours later, she woke to find the world outside her window changed. The rain was gone. In its place was a thick snow that had turned the landscape white. The engineer had also reduced the speed of the train to a crawl, afraid that he might hit an unseen stalled train. By morning, Sara's train was five hours behind schedule and had not even reached Albany.

Sara and the other passengers watched with growing alarm as the train plowed ahead cautiously. The wind was whirling the already fallen snow into tornadolike snow devils or pushing it into bigger and bigger wavelike drifts. Two miles outside of Albany, the engineer spotted a monstrous snowdrift ahead and made an instantaneous decision. He pushed the throttle forward, hoping to smash his train through.

There was no warning for the passengers to brace themselves. When the train hit the snow, Sara was looking out the window, while other people were reading, chatting, snoozing, or strolling about the car. The engine sliced into the bank of snow easily, but then it seemed as if a giant hand had clamped its fingers around it. The train stopped so abruptly that the parlor car leaped from the tracks and passengers went flying. The engine was almost entirely covered with snow and stuck fast.

None of the passengers was seriously hurt, but that didn't mean they were out of danger. The crash had toppled over the iron stoves used to heat the cars, spewing red-hot coals in every direction. Several men tried to stamp out the flames, but the fire spread quickly, jumping from the carpet to the drapes to the ceiling. In a matter of seconds, one end of the beautiful parlor car was engulfed in flames, and passengers were scrambling to get out the door at the opposite end.

Sara was dragged to her feet by a gentleman passenger and led to the exit. Before leaving, she grabbed her fashionable Empress Eugénie hat with its long red feather. All passengers and crew — forty-seven men and five women — escaped and now found themselves in a driving snowstorm, watching the train being consumed by flames.

It was obvious that they couldn't stand out there very long. But in which direction should they go? The conductor pointed up the tracks and said Albany was only two miles away. It was so close, he told them, that on a clear day they would be able to see the church spires from where they stood. So they divided up into groups of four and set off, with the train crew breaking a trail for the others.

At first, the journey went smoothly because the snow was only a few feet deep beyond the big drift and the trail easy to follow. Within minutes, however, the spirit of adventure vanished. Most of the travelers weren't dressed for the bitter cold, and their leather-bottomed shoes made walking difficult. As the snow became deeper, walking grew more and more fatiguing.

Sara floundered along, trying to keep up with her group. At one

Many trains derailed while attempting to plow through giant snowdrifts. Workers in Naugatuck, Connecticut, have dug out this particular wreck, and now must haul it back onto the tracks before passenger service can resume. (FAIRFIELD HISTORICAL SOCIETY)

point, she stumbled and found herself stuck in snow that was waist-deep. A man came back to pull her out and she went on, exhausted. Later, the men helped her as best as they could and each took a turn carrying her. Soon, however, they found their own strength failing and their thoughts completely taken up with their own survival. They set her on her feet and urged her to keep walking. Then they disappeared into the blinding snow ahead.

Sara was alone now, with nobody to call on for help. The wind slapped at her face and roughly shoved her around. Her long blond hair froze, and she lost feeling in her toes and fingertips. Her mouth was open, gasping for air, and she probably closed her eyes during her final few steps.

The body closes down as hypothermia sets in, and it seems a little like going to sleep. The senses grow numb, pain begins to recede, and the thought process becomes cloudy and unfocused. If Sara called out for help, it was a feeble call. If she tried to walk, her legs did not respond.

At some point, Sara ran out of strength entirely and stopped moving. Snow and ice clung to her clothes, hair, and face as if she were a statue in a park. Then the icy figure toppled over backward. Her will to struggle, to push herself up and keep moving, was gone. She lay there as if she were on the softest of featherbeds.

Immediately, snow began to cover her face and body as well as the hat she had clung to throughout her ordeal. Soon, only the red feather poked through the snow, and then it, too, disappeared. The storm was only a few hours old, really, just a baby, and yet it had already claimed dozens of victims.

THREE

THE LAND IS AN OCEAN OF SNOW

On Monday, March 12, people from Delaware on up to Maine, and inland as far as the Mississippi River, woke to discover a white and hostile visitor lurking outside. A blizzard was rattling their windowpanes and piling up snow against their doors.

A blizzard is defined as any storm where snow is accompanied by temperatures of 20 degrees Fahrenheit or lower, plus winds of at least 35 miles per hour. During the Blizzard of 1888, temperatures often went below zero, and winds were clocked at 75 to 85 miles per hour. Many newspapers nicknamed the storm the Great White Hurricane.

The exact origin of the word *blizzard* is disputed and debated. The English claim it came from the common Midland expression "may I be blizzarded," which, roughly translated, means "I'll be damned." The notion is that the astonished speaker has been knocked over by an icy blast. Others say the word is derived from the German *blitzartig*, which means "lightning-like."

In the United States, some insist the word came from an old western phrase "to be blizzarded," or struck many times by violent punches.

A few curious individuals experience a snowy scene on Joralemon Street, Brooklyn. (NEW-YORK HISTORICAL SOCIETY)

And we do know that in Tennessee and Kentucky, the word is used to refer to a period of intense cold, even without wind or snow.

Whatever its origin, the word *blizzard* certainly fit what was happening to the northeastern coast that morning. As temperatures plummeted, the wet snow changed into tiny, sharp particles of ice that ripped at any exposed skin. A Philadelphia resident remembered how "the snow would follow breath into his lungs and fill them with water, nearly choking him."

An Albany *Journal* reporter struggled through the howling wind and snow to his paper's offices where he wrote: "In truth the land is an ocean of snow. . . . The city looked dead and was literally buried."

His city may have appeared lifeless, but in fact there was a great deal of activity going on. Monday was the beginning of the week, which meant work and school for hundreds of thousands of people. Bank presidents, chambermaids, store owners, factory workers, telegraph operators, students, schoolteachers and principals, Western Union messengers, blacksmiths, and newspaper deliverers alike set out that morning just as they did on any other workday. This was true in big cities such as Albany, Boston, Buffalo, and New York, and in the many smaller towns and villages in between.

Milkman William Brubacker was one such person. When he awoke at 1:30 A.M. Monday morning, a hard, vicious snow was pelting his house in downtown New York City. But Brubacker never hesitated. His customers expected to find their bottles of milk and cream waiting as always, and he had no intention of disappointing them.

After hitching up his horse and wagon, Brubacker went to the Hudson River, where he crossed to Jersey City on a ferry. There he met the milk train, loaded his wagon, and returned to New York City to begin his deliveries. By this time, it was 5 A.M. and Brubacker was already two hours behind schedule.

Dutifully, he followed his usual route, going up one slick cobblestone street and down another, making every stop just as he would on a normal morning. Often, the milk boxes were hidden by drifts of snow and sealed tight by ice, so William had to dig them out and chip away till the lids opened.

At 10 A.M. that morning, he had only covered about half his normal route when painfully cold ears and exhaustion forced him to stop at a saloon to warm up. He gulped down a glass of whiskey and was preparing to leave when the bartender told him he looked awful. "He made me walk the floor for ten minutes and I had another drink. I began to realize myself that I did not stop any too soon."

At the time, a glass or two (or more) of whiskey was considered the best medicine to fight off cold and frostbite, and was liberally administered to men, women, and children. Never mind that it often left the patient intoxicated, or that the illusion of warmth the liquor provided often prompted a drunk to stagger back out into the storm.

Reluctantly, but wisely, Brubacker turned his horse and wagon around and went home, where he stayed for the next four days. Later, he would recall that long before he understood the danger of the storm,

A horse and carriage struggles along 14th Street and Fifth Avenue during the early part of the storm. (NEW-YORK HISTORICAL SOCIETY)

his horse had turned toward the stable three times. "He had more sense than I," William concluded.

Another group who made it to work were the men of the New York City Weather Station. Sergeant Francis Long was the first at the station, but soon his boss, Chief Dunn, and all the others arrived.

The day before, they had to deal with no communications from Washington or any of the other local weather stations. Today, they found that the machine to measure wind velocity, the anemometer, had frozen stiff. Fixing the instrument seemed out of the question. It was screwed to the top of a four-inch-wide pole that was affixed to the rooftop tower, nearly 200 feet above the sidewalk. Chief Dunn estimated that the wind gusts were "75 miles an hour in a driving spiculum of snow and ice."

Sergeant Long stepped forward and volunteered to repair the anemometer. At first, Dunn refused to let Long risk his life, saying, "You are too heavy a man. The pole will snap and I will be responsible for a dead man." "Sir," Long replied, "it will be at my own risk."

After a few more minutes of discussion, Chief Dunn relented. "[Long] climbed that slim pole without any support," Dunn would say in a report, "adjusted the instrument and replaced some wiring with one hand. . . . The wind pressure was so great that it was most difficult for one to stand up, even by holding on, and impossible to get one's breath if facing the wind. Long was nearly frozen, but still he kept on until the instrument was in proper working order. It was a most heroic act. . . . The principal record of the storm would have been lost had it not been for Francis Long."

Long never wrote about this incident, and he never spoke very much about it, either. He continued working at the weather station for another twenty-eight years, and eventually became chief forecaster. For

The railroad cuts into New York City trapped many trains and their passengers. Here, a long line of passenger trains sit helpless as snow piles up around them. (AUTHOR'S COLLECTION)

Sergeant Long, climbing a wobbling pole in the face of a blizzard was simply a part of his job.

Habit and duty were some of the reasons so many people risked death to show up for work. Everyone at the weather station, for instance, was a member of the U.S. Army; it was their sworn duty to be there. Add to this the fact that a true blizzard rarely visited the East Coast area. People simply did not understand the dangers it posed. Many "hardy individualists" — almost all of them men — looked at the storm as an inconvenience that sheer determination could overcome. Former senator Roscoe Conkling certainly did.

Conkling was a tall, powerfully built man who was an imposing figure even at age fifty-eight. He'd been through some nasty political battles during his career, so a little snow and wind wasn't going to stop

him from walking the twenty-five blocks from his home to the courthouse.

Only no one else showed up in court — not the judge, nor the plaintiffs, nor the defendants; not even the other lawyers. Disgusted, Conkling left the courthouse and trudged off to his law office to write letters.

If a few — like Long and Conkling — defied the storm without much trouble, many more felt its bite. A. C. Chadbourne had left Boston the night before on the New Haven Railroad with his business partner, headed to New York City. "I awoke at 7 a.m. . . . and found the train stalled in deep snow at about 127th Street. I got out the car door and saw a line of cars and trains stalled ahead of me as far as one could see."

Chadbourne and his partner decided to abandon the train. "There were some stone steps thoroughly snow covered leading . . . to the sidewalk. Down these steps we slid, landing in a snowbank at the bottom which buried us alive. Great drifts were piled six to eight feet high in many places and the air was so full of snow it was difficult to see where one was going."

At this point, they should have sought a local hotel to wait out the storm. They were eighty-nine blocks away from the hotel where they usually stayed, a distance of over four miles. But they were focused on the important business deal they hoped to make that afternoon and had no intention of being late. So they pressed on.

They hadn't gone very far when they came upon one of the few clothing stores open that morning. There they bought six pairs of socks and two large handkerchiefs. "We put on the thin woolen socks," Chadbourne remembered. "[Then] we pulled the coarse woolen socks over our shoes, tucked our trousers in them and tied the socks around our ankles with a cord to keep the snow from working down into our feet. We tied the handkerchiefs over our heads and under our chins and then pulled our silk hats as far down our heads as possible. The two other pairs of socks we pulled on over our gloves in place of mittens. . . ."

Their outfits looked ridiculous, but they did protect the covered areas from the numbing cold. The wind was another matter altogether. As they set off again, Chadbourne recalled, "There was a heavy gale blowing. I remember seeing my partner blown helplessly almost a block, his travel ended by falling into a snow drift which completely covered him."

After rescuing him, the two continued their stumbling, sometimes tumbling journey down Third Avenue. Strong gusts of wind tore wooden gates from their posts and store signs from buildings. At one point, Chadbourne and his friend turned a corner and "narrowly escaped death . . . [when] a wooden fence was blown on us while wallowing in a deep drift."

Many other things were being blown about as well. Like most cities back then, New York had no antilitter laws, so newspapers, household trash, bits and pieces of debris, broken glass, and ashes were routinely tossed into the gutter without thought. Add to this a daily deposit of two and one-half million pounds of manure and 60,000 gallons of urine from the city's 60,000 horses! All of this garbage hardened into chunks that were picked up by the wind and slapped into travelers' faces.

Whenever possible, Chadbourne and his partner would duck around the corner of a building to find a bit of shelter from the wind. Despite such energy-saving measures, the men were barely able to stay upright as they neared their destination, the Gedney House on 38th Street. "I distinctly remember being blown down twice while crossing Broadway and crawling through the snow on my hands and knees [to the opposite] sidewalk."

Once safe inside the hotel, Chadbourne saw for the first time how the storm had transformed them. "My partner looked terribly, his mustache was a wabbly cake of ice which had pounded on his chin as he walked until [it] was bleeding. My face was scratched, red as a lobster, my eyebrows were frozen and my chin was resting on a cake of snowy ice packed between the top of my overcoat and my bandanna handkerchief."

While Chadbourne and his partner had chosen to brave the storm, most people who attempted to get to their workplaces on Blizzard Monday did so out of fear. There were few laws in place that spelled out a worker's rights or protected him or her in any way. Business owners and their managers assumed that if they could get to work, all of their

Two men lean into the fierce wind as they make their way through the wire-infested, lonely streets near Wall Street.
(NEW-YORK HISTORICAL SOCIETY)

employees should show up as well. Workers were routinely fined for being late or absent.

Job security had become even more fragile in 1888, when a severe economic depression resulted in the nationwide layoff of more than 100,000 workers. Those lucky enough to have jobs knew they could be replaced very easily. Fourteen-year-old L. B. Aspen walked over sixty blocks to his job. "I did not want to take a chance of losing it," he would explain. "Jobs those days were hard to get — even office-boy jobs."

Eighteen-year-old May Morrow would have preferred to stay inside her warm boardinghouse room on West 47th Street, but she was fairly new at her job and insecure. Besides, she was the telegraph operator for a small wholesale chemical company and vital in the day-to-day operation of that business.

So May left home extra early that morning and managed to catch a slow-moving elevated train — one of the last still running — at Ninth Avenue. The ride seemed to take forever, but May managed to arrive just a few minutes late. No one else showed up for work that day except the head of the firm, Mr. Garrigues. May wasn't upset by the inconvenience; by showing up, she had proved to her boss that she was a dedicated worker.

James Algeo had felt the power of the storm the night before, but he still made sure he got to his job at the American Bank Note Company on time. Only forty other workers of the 1,200 employees braved the weather that day. Over at the Customs House, one-third of the workers arrived, almost all of them women. The employment of female customs inspectors was still in the experimental phase at the time and many of the women felt their jobs were vulnerable.

At the Singer Sewing Machine factory in Elizabeth, New Jersey, 1,800 of the 3,200 workers arrived before the late whistle sounded.

Among those at work that day were seventeen-year-old James Marshall and two of his friends, Alexander Bennett and Charles Lee. All three lived on Staten Island and traveled from there to Elizabeth in a jointly owned rowboat.

On Blizzard Monday, they met as always at the boat landing and set off across Newark Bay, a journey of about one-half mile. They had made the crossing in all sorts of weather, so the hardy young men were not about to let the snow stop them. They were 150 feet from shore when it became clear that this was no ordinary storm. The wind batted their little boat around and the choppy waters splashed them until their faces began to ice up. They were about to turn back when the wind shifted and actually helped push them across the Bay. They arrived at the factory on time.

Even young children wouldn't let the obvious power of the storm get in their way. In Brooklyn, ten-year-old Rufus Billings announced at breakfast that he intended to go to school. His parents tried to talk him out of this reckless adventure, and even hid his boots, but young Rufus was determined. He found his boots and plunged out into the storm before his worried parents could stop him.

A dozen other students were already at the school when Rufus arrived. The only problem was that the door was locked. No adults had made it — not the principal, teachers, or the janitor. Still, these children had no intention of giving up. They huddled at the front door for an hour and only went home when the principal finally appeared and officially proclaimed school closed for the day.

Another very determined child was ten-year-old Sam Strong, who lived in Harlem with his aunt and uncle, Mr. and Mrs. Charles Green. Sam didn't have to fight and argue to go outside. His aunt actually gave him a list of items she wanted him to buy at Brady's notion store before

FRANK LESLIE'S ILLUSTRATED BLIZZARD NEWSPAPER

No. 1,697.—Vol. LXVI.] NEW YORK—FOR THE WEEK ENDING MARCH 24, 1888. [Price, 10 Cents.

Hats and umbrellas go flying and pedestrians twist and fall in the hurricane-force winds produced by the Great Blizzard. The only thing standing tall and straight is a statue in the background. (Museum of the City of New York) going on to school. Among the things he was to get were whalebones, dressmaker's chalk, and a large needle, so his aunt could sew herself a new corset.

Sam glanced out the front window and saw a man get blown over by the wind. He also noticed that the front gate was completely covered by a five-foot-tall snowdrift. When he said something about this to his aunt, she made him wear his high rubber boots, a heavy overcoat, woolen cap, gloves, and a muffler. "There," she said as she buttoned up his coat, "you could go to the North Pole in that outfit. Hurry up now, so you won't be late for school."

At first, Sam liked the experience of being outside in a wild storm, fighting his way through belt-high snow and fending off the wind. His aunt and uncle had instilled in him a strong sense of self-reliance and duty. He had been told to go to the store and then to school, so he was going to do both, no matter what the consequences.

Several blocks later, Sam came face-to-face with the violence of the blizzard. As he was crossing an intersection, the wind was on him like a wild animal. It picked him up and tossed him into a deep snowdrift.

Sam struggled and clawed to get free of the snow, but he was in over his head. The more he moved, the more snow fell on top of him. He shrieked for help, but no one heard him above the wind's mighty roar. His boyish romp had turned into a frightening trap in just seconds. Finally, just as his strength was about to give out, a policeman came along and yanked him free. "You hadn't ought to be out in this, Sonny," he recalled the policeman telling him. "You go straight home."

But Sam didn't go home. More determined than ever, he pressed on, going down 125th Street, past abandoned wagons and carriages. A cable car being pulled by four horses struggled along at a feeble pace, while the few other people out that morning were hunkered over against the icy gusts. "When I could get down out of the cutting wind behind a snowdrift, I was all right," the boy recalled, "but traveling took every ounce of power in my body."

When he finally reached Brady's, he discovered it closed, the front door and window covered completely by a giant snowdrift. Instead of giving up, Sam continued along the street for several blocks, hoping to discover a store — any store — open. There were none.

At this point, he stopped a fellow traveler to see if the man knew where he could purchase a corset needle. The man had no idea where to get the needle, but he did teach Sam something else. "[I] learned a few new and attractive profane expressions to add to my already fair vocabulary of cuss words, and with his help I about-faced and started the homeward trek."

If anything, his return journey proved more treacherous. The drifts seemed to have grown enormously in height; the snow seemed sharper, the wind more cutting. Sam, like thousands of others, would later come to realize that as fatigue set in, obstacles he had handled fairly easily before were now much harder to deal with. Six times Sam got stuck in the snow and six times he had to be pulled to safety. Finally, at around noon, he clawed his way up his front stairs and tumbled into the vestibule.

Neither his aunt nor his uncle — who had stayed home from work — said anything harsh to the boy. It was Sam who was upset. "Although I had fought the snow for more than four hours, I had failed in my mission. There were many tears. . . . I [went to] bed with glass bottles filled with hot water, a big slug of raw whiskey, and some food, and I was asleep, not waking until night and then only for more food and drink. I was exhausted."

THIS IS ALL SO OVERWHELMING

Chauncey Depew arrived at the Grand Central Depot on Monday with one goal in mind. As president of the New York Central Railroad, he was determined to keep his trains running. What he found that morning did not make him happy.

Normally, Grand Central was the busiest terminal in North America, with hundreds of trains scheduled to arrive and depart every day. On Blizzard Monday, the immense building was uncomfortably quiet. A New York *Sun* reporter noted that "The interior of the station and the yard immediately outside . . . were as silent as the grave. . . . No sound was audible in the great structure save that of the moaning wind."

Upstairs in his office another sort of silence greeted Depew. The telegraph lines — which usually clicked away with reports on the weather and other related railroad information — were all dead quiet. Depew had no idea where his trains were or of the extent of the problem the storm was causing.

Depew was not the sort of man to lounge in his office fretting. He had succeeded the late William H. Vanderbilt as president of the railroad, and Vanderbilt was a man who did not let anyone — or any-thing — stand in his way. Those were big shoes to fill, but Depew was determined to battle the snow head-on.

It was obvious that somewhere up the tracks a train or trains were stuck and blocking all other inbound trains. Workers were sent out on foot to find out where those trains were. Next, Depew began consider-ing the best way to clear the track.

Obviously, the snow was too deep for an engine to simply push its way through. Otherwise, some of the early-morning trains would have made it to the station. Depew also assumed that the plows the railroad had were too small to do the job. That left Depew only one option — moving the snow by hand.

In the railyards just behind Grand Central Depot, a crew of Italian laborers shovel snow into coal cars for disposal. (NEW-YORK HISTORICAL SOCIETY)

After consulting his assistants and several experienced trainmen, it was decided to hire day laborers to do the job. Despite the fact that shoveling snow in a raging blizzard was hard, dangerous work that paid very little — just $1.20 for a ten-hour day — finding men was easy.

At the time, between 5,000 and 10,000 immigrants were pouring into the United States every day, almost all of them poor and desperate for any sort of work. In the past, the Irish would have answered Depew's call. But in 1888, the largest number of immigrants came from Italy.

Messengers went into the Italian neighborhoods, stopping at church parish houses, charity missions, saloons, and other gathering places to spread the word. Within a few hours, an army of 1,000 Italian workers had been assembled, most of them wearing the thin coats and gloves they had brought from Italy.

The train closest to Grand Central was the Boston *Express*, now imprisoned in a mountain of snow at the 59th Street cut, some fifteen blocks away. A cut is any section of exposed track that runs below the level of the surrounding ground, for example, where the track slices through a hill. Blowing snow fell into these long, narrow slits and piled up, sometimes filling the entire cut.

Six hundred Italian workers descended on the 59th Street cut and began hacking away at the frozen mound of snow. Some removed snow from around the engine, which was almost completely buried, while the rest began clearing the tracks ahead.

Meanwhile, up the tracks at the very top of New York City, 400 other workers faced an even greater challenge — freeing trains at the Spuyten Duyvil cut. This particular cut was 500 feet long and 150 feet deep and had a sharp curve in the middle of it. A commuter train had hit a wall of white at 6:30 A.M. and been buried ever since. The Peekskill local with eight cars stopped behind this first train, then came two long

This page from a special "Blizzard Edition" shows how the storm tied up all forms of transportation.

trains carrying passengers from the West. In no time at all, eight trains were stuck fast one behind the other in a line over a mile long.

The rock walls were tall and close together at the Spuyten cut, which made digging a difficult chore. In addition, with so little space on the sides, snow and ice had to be carried outside the cut before it could be thrown clear of the tracks.

The Italian laborers went at the snow with great energy, chipping and hacking at it as best they could. The wind shrieked and roared between the walls of the cut and was so strong that at times it tore the wide shovels from the workers' hands.

After clearing eight feet of track, they hit icy snow so solid that the shovels bounced off harmlessly. Picks and axes were brought in, but another hour of assaulting the iced snow produced only 15 feet more of cleared track. No matter how quickly the men worked, snow cascading over the edge of the cut continually covered up the track.

Word about the losing battle was sent back to an increasingly frustrated Depew. Besides the ghost of Vanderbilt to nag him about his failure to keep the trains running, another force was being heard from as well. At around noon, Frederick Van Wyck, a wealthy friend of Depew's, sent a note saying he was trapped just outside the city, and asking if Depew could get his train unstuck. In addition, Harrison Twombly (the son-in-law of Mr. Vanderbilt) was sending frantic messages that the 4 A.M. milk train had failed to appear and that his children needed milk urgently.

Depew knew that this was just the beginning of the complaints. As the New York *Sun* reporter would write, "Most of the unfortunates who were caught in the local trains were wealthy brokers and businessmen, and [Mr. Depew] smiled sadly as he thought of the wrath that would come down upon him from these patrons of his road."

As the snow piles up on the street in front of the Scientific American Building, horsecars, wagons, and pedestrians struggle to keep moving. (AUTHOR'S COLLECTION)

Depew fretted and fumed throughout the day, but it did little good. One of the greatest railroads in the world had come to a complete halt. Of the forty regular mail trains, only one came into New York City that day. No milk nor meat nor coal shipments arrived at all.

When a reporter asked about the condition of the tracks, Depew finally exploded: "There isn't any road — it has disappeared. There are eighteen trains between here and Yonkers and there is no way of getting them down as yet. . . . The engines are absolutely snowed under." Depew sat back in his chair and finally admitted, "There is no way of telling when trains will move again. This is all so overwhelming. . . ."

Depew might have taken some comfort in knowing that he wasn't the only one stopped by the storm. All forms of transportation in New York City were grinding to a snowy halt. The four elevated trains were shut down during the morning out of fear that ice and wind would eventually send a train over the edge. Fifteen thousand commuters, plus the train crews, were marooned high above the streets in unheated wooden coaches.

The horse-drawn streetcars did their very best to keep moving during the early hours. But fighting the deepening snow and slippery paving stones proved too much, even when four and six horses were used. Most drivers realized they were beaten before noon. Once this decision was made, they unhitched their horses and led them back to the barn, abandoning cars — and passengers — on the empty streets.

By late afternoon, the only form of ground transportation available came from private individuals with wagons, coaches, or sleighs. These men drove their exhausted animals hard to keep them plowing through the chest-high snow. Dozens of horses died that day as a result of the abuse. The possibility of a dead horse did not stop drivers from whipping their animals on. It might cost one hundred dollars to replace a horse, a sizable amount in those days. But by noon, the charge for a trip of two or three blocks had gone up to fifty dollars. Drivers pocketed the money and put their animals at risk.

Many New Yorkers knew that this breakdown in the transportation system shouldn't have happened. One such person was the editor of *Scientific American*, Alfred Ely Beach.

Thirty-nine years before, Beach had grown frustrated by the traffic congestion he encountered every day on his way to work. One study by the *New York Tribune* revealed that over 1,000 vehicles passed by the corner of Chambers Street and Broadway *every hour, for thirteen straight hours.* Traveling on a sunny day was so slow that the *Tribune* complained: "We can travel from New York half-way to Philadelphia in less time than the length of Broadway." Whenever it rained or snowed, travel came to a virtual halt.

Beach's idea was simple and logical: If the streets aboveground were jammed, why not travel underground? Beach's subway train was to run the entire length of Broadway. "The cars," Beach promised, "will stop ten seconds at every corner — thus performing the trip up and down, including stops, in about an hour."

The idea was revolutionary and many people and newspapers championed it. Unfortunately, New York City was controlled politically by William Marcy ("Boss") Tweed and his allies, and they crushed every piece of legislation for Beach's subway. Why? Because Tweed as the city's commissioner of public works had grown rich and powerful by extorting money from the horsecar and street railroad companies. He had no intention of undermining his chief source of income.

Beach spent two decades trying to win approval for his subway. He even built a 300-foot-long test tunnel and car that attracted 400,000 paying customers in 1870. Even with this obvious success, Beach could not overcome his opponents. As he stared out his window on Blizzard Monday at the abandoned coaches and streetcars, Alfred Ely Beach wondered how things might have been different if his subway system were in operation.

If traveling aboveground in New York City was nearly impossible, just getting onto the island was becoming more and more difficult by the minute. The thirty-five ferry lines linking New York City with New Jersey, Long Island, Staten Island, and Brooklyn struggled valiantly to maintain commuter service. The falling snow cut visibility to a few hundred feet, and large chunks of ice clogged the rivers and landing slips. Still, the sturdy side-wheel ferryboats chugged back and forth all morning, even though whitecaps in the Hudson made for a rough ride. "The river rose like an ocean," one commuter mumbled after a wave-tossed ride.

During normal rush hours, ferries came and went at five-minute intervals. On Blizzard Monday, it was not uncommon to wait an hour or longer. As the day wore on, many ferry captains found they could not force their vessels through the thickening ice, and were forced to give up. One ferry lost power and was swept down the Hudson to the bay where it nearly capsized, while another collided with a schooner, killing one woman passenger.

The larger, more powerful ferries continued their crossings throughout the day, though with increasing danger. At one point, passengers on a Staten Island ferry looked up to see the schooner *Mary Heitman* bouncing wildly along the water toward them. The five crewmen of the schooner clung to the railings helplessly. After barely missing the ferry, the *Mary Heitman* continued her mad journey to the open ocean and neither boat nor crew were ever seen again. As evening approached, only a few of the largest ferries were still running.

With railroad service suspended and most ferries docked, only one sure route into New York City remained open — the Brooklyn Bridge. In the morning, police barred carriages and wagons from the bridge, fearing the high winds might send a vehicle over the edge and into the river below. The cable car that ran up the middle of the bridge labored to make trips across the structure, as did hundreds and hundreds of walking commuters.

Early in the afternoon, ice caused the cable car to jump the tracks as it approached the New York City side. Workmen struggled to get the cable car back on track, but it took them so long that a winch froze, putting a stop to the cable service.

The station and outside platform were jammed with commuters impatient to pay their five-cent fare to get across to Brooklyn. When they learned that the cable car would not be running anymore, they began to push forward and a riot nearly took place.

At around the same time, police were growing more concerned about the effect the storm might have on the bridge itself. While the bridge

With the bridge trains stalled and the ferryboats blocked, the only way for these rugged Brooklynites to get home was to hike across the Brooklyn Bridge.
(New-York Historical Society)

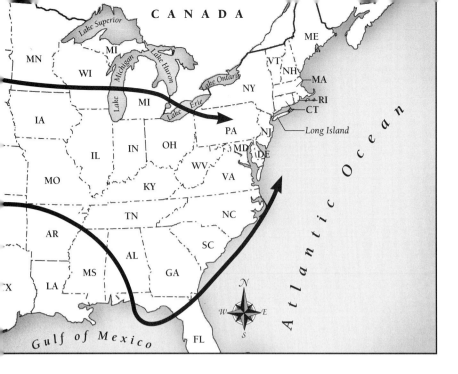

The northern storm hadn't really moved much in twenty-four hours, which meant it was still pumping frigid air into the northern Atlantic states. The southern storm with its strong winds and moisture had already rushed north and collided with the cold air from Canada, producing a mighty blizzard.

had withstood many storms in its five years of existence, the concept of suspension bridges was relatively new and untested. Just ten years before, a suspension bridge in Dundee, Scotland, had collapsed during a winter storm, killing seventy-five people. Worried that the weight of ice and snow and thousands of people might cause a similar disaster here, the police officially closed the Brooklyn Bridge to all travel. Not only was the island of New York City isolated from the rest of the world, but everyone on it was trapped.

In general, people living on farms and in small rural towns fared much better than city folk during the blizzard. Those in the countryside were used to being isolated, especially during snowstorms. Winters of the past — and the wisdom and training of the parents and grandparents of these country people — had taught them to be prepared.

Most farm families had an ample wood supply piled just outside the back door. Root cellars contained potatoes, turnips, carrots, and apples, while smoked meats hung from the walls. There would be shelves lined with jars of preserved fruits and vegetables, sacks of wheat and corn flour, plus casks of homemade wine and apple cider. Even if they were completely cut off, a farm family could survive for days and weeks with little trouble. Yet the blizzard managed to test many of these people as well.

In Tidewater, Virginia, a farm couple watched with growing alarm as a nearby river overflowed its banks and water began seeping under their front door. As the ground floor filled up, the husband and wife retreated upstairs, bringing along their ten pigs and twenty chickens. This oinking, clucking group would live together on the crowded second floor until the water receded four days later.

A young teacher in southern Vermont wasn't surprised in the least to begin classes that morning with every seat occupied. Deep snow was fairly common in the area and the local people weren't about to let a little bad weather stand in the way of their children's education. So this teacher taught lessons through the morning and into the early afternoon.

He grew worried when the storm increased in ferocity at noon, and then alarmed when he saw that a snowdrift was almost up to the windowsill on one side of the building. He decided to dismiss classes early, though he hesitated to send his pupils out on their own. Some of the children were so young and small that the snow on the ground was already over their heads.

His solution to the problem was as straightforward and practical as the people in the area were: He tied a rope to all fourteen of his students, with him and several of the larger students in front to break a trail. Then he led them out into the storm, going from one child's home to the next until each had been delivered safely. His school day finally over, he went home to milk and feed his cows. It would be three weeks before the roads were clear enough to resume classes.

This schoolmaster and his charges were fortunate. They were young and healthy, so their bodies could withstand the battering of the storm. Others weren't so lucky. Sunday's rain and Monday's snow had kept Sam Randall away from his fields, but it didn't free him of all farm chores. Late Monday afternoon, as the light dimmed, the elderly man got ready to make yet another trip from his house to the barn. Blizzard or not, the cows needed milking and the other animals had to be cared for.

He put on his heavy coat and hat, took a hurricane lamp for light, and began plowing through the waist-high snow to the barn. He was a hearty man for his age, used to the rigors of farm life and manual labor. Yet the force of the wind combined with the effort of moving his legs forward soon wore him down.

The wind swirled the snow up and around and into Randall's face. He was leaning into the wind, trying to pull his legs along, when he slipped and floundered ahead a step or two. The lantern dropped from his hand and then he fell face first into the snow. He struggled to get to his feet, but the wind and snow pushed and pounded at him and kept him from getting up. He died just 30 feet from the warmth of his own house, surrounded by darkness and waves of snow.

Across the Long Island Sound, in the village of Montville, Connecticut, another drama was unfolding. The Chapell family sensed immediately on Monday morning that the storm raging outside was dangerous, but they had provisions to last many days and weren't much alarmed. It didn't even bother them that Mr. Chapell had spent the night at his ailing mother's farm a half mile away. Mrs. Chapell knew how to run a farm — and keep her four sons busy — in any kind of weather.

Everything went along smoothly until word arrived that Father was himself ill with some sort of fever and asking that his wife come at once. Since her oldest son, Alfred, was doing chores in the barn, Mrs. Chapell put her second oldest son, George, in charge of his two little brothers, Gurdon, nine, and Legrand, four. Then she set off for Grandma's house.

The three boys in the house did their best to stay occupied, popping corn, playing with toys, and chasing the cat from room to room. By midafternoon, boredom had set in and George announced that he was going to Grandma's. Gurdon and Legrand begged to go along, but George had had enough baby-sitting to last him awhile and told them no. George was in such a hurry to get away that he didn't even bother going to the barn to tell Alfred what he planned to do.

The two little boys watched at the window as George disappeared into a wall of swirling white, then they turned back to their play. Almost immediately, the stillness of the house began to make them uneasy. The ticking of the clock seemed loud and sinister, and the snow hitting the windows sounded as if someone were trying to break in. When Legrand asked what they should do next, Gurdon answered, "I know, we'll go and surprise Mother and Father."

They bundled up snugly, then stepped outside. The force of the storm made them hesitate on the front porch. On a clear day, they could see their grandmother's house from there, even though it was two fields and a pasture away. Today, they couldn't even see the front gate.

Gurdon wasn't about to give up. He had been to Grandma's house many times and knew that only a couple of low stone walls stood between them. So he took firm hold of his little brother's hand and waded into the snow.

Later, Alfred would finish up his chores in the barn and return to find the house empty and dark. No alarm bells went off in his head. He assumed that everyone had gone to Grandma's together and would stay there that night. He might have checked with his parents, but, of course, there was no telephone service as yet in their rural area. It would not be until the next morning that anyone realized Gurdon and Legrand were missing.

By nightfall on Monday, the center of the storm had barely moved, and icy winds of hurricane force swept across an area from Virginia up to Nova Scotia, Canada. The wind was so powerful that in Liberty, New York, the local train station had its roof entirely ripped off. Down in Baltimore, the gale blew the water completely out of the harbor, while the Delaware River seemed to part in two near Philadelphia.

The heavy snowfall continued and temperatures began dropping. At 6 P.M. that night, thermometers in Northfield, Vermont, dipped to 4 degrees Fahrenheit, while farther south in Central Park, the temperature recorded was 12 degrees Fahrenheit — and falling.

Hundreds of cows stranded in distant pastures froze to death that night, while thousands of birds nesting in the decorative trim of buildings succumbed to the freezing cold and fell to the streets below. A guest of the New York City Hotel at 23rd Street looked out his window and saw "a veritable rain of sparrows falling dead from the eaves of nearby buildings." At the Old London Building, 500 dead birds would be swept up when the storm was over.

The astonishing thing to remember is, that even as night came on and the storm worsened, tens of thousands of workers faced another adventure. They still had to make their way home.

FIVE

I WENT MAGNIFICENTLY ALONG

As darkness closed in, the majority of people chose safety over comfort and stayed inside wherever possible. In New York City, train stations, ferry landings, churches, police stations, firehouses, and mission houses were packed tight. Every hotel was stuffed full, with five or more people sharing a room and others sleeping in the lobby, hallways, and even closets. One elderly woman had her bed made up in a bathtub and was grateful for her accommodations.

In the countryside, people sought shelter in isolated churches, barns, or chicken houses. Most lucky travelers would stumble up to the first house he or she came to and be welcomed inside without hesitation.

Sometimes a gracious home owner found himself or herself in an awkward situation. One Connecticut farmwife opened her door to six wayward travelers, but discovered she didn't have enough food for a decent meal. Instead of disappointing her guests, she went outside and gathered up a heaping basket of frozen sparrows. Dinner was a bit gamy, but no one complained.

Divinity student John Marshall would have traded places willingly with any of the Connecticut sparrow eaters. The train he had taken out of Lewes had been packed tight in snow all day, and he and the other four passengers had spent the time talking, playing cards, and writing letters. Reading his Bible had helped John pass a number of hours.

Luckily for John, his train had a large supply of coal for its stove. Many other stranded train travelers found themselves shivering and miserable as coal ran out. The most daring individuals would abandon the shelter of their cars to seek out the nearest village. By and large, train travelers stayed put and found creative ways to keep their stove fires burning — which usually meant burning the wooden seats, car paneling, and wall ornaments. When wood grew scarce, passengers often raided the baggage cars and burned crates, suitcases, and, in one case, the U.S. Mail.

Food was another matter. Like many travelers, John Marshall had

In general, no one bothered to remove snow until a storm ended. One exception was the horsecar companies that battled unsuccessfully to keep their most important routes open. Here, a plow pulled by ten horses clears a busy intersection. (AUTHOR'S COLLECTION)

brought along a small satchel of food to snack on during the trip. When these scant supplies were gone, hunger pangs took over.

Gnawing on ice might fill the stomach for a while, but eventually that stomach would demand real food. Long-distance trains often carried supplies of food and milk, and these would be broken into and consumed. A few railroad companies sent out rescue parties with supplies for their stranded passengers. Trains stuck in the more remote areas often did not see help for two or three days. This lack of concern prompted the Providence (Rhode Island) *Journal* to complain, "It seems that the [train] company intends to . . . let the travelling public work out its own salvation."

John Marshall knew firsthand that the storm outside his train cars was a killing force one person couldn't long endure. He stayed put and endured his growling stomach. He would probably have agreed with the sentiments of a conductor, identified only as Mr. DeWolfe, who was at that same moment trapped in rural Connecticut. "The car was warm and tight," Mr. DeWolfe noted, "but the air began to be very heavy and oppressive. It was like a tomb."

While the majority of people chose to stay out of the storm, the need to get home drove thousands of people right into its sharp teeth. May Morrow had spent the day copying letters, filing, and straightening up the office. Every so often, she would stop what she was doing to watch the storm.

Up and down the street, the poles carrying telegraph, telephone, and electric wires had snapped in two and several had crashed through windows. Once, a strange noise drew her to the window, and she and her boss saw a horse tangled in live high-voltage wires with sparks dancing along its head and neck.

New York City was littered with hundreds of fallen poles and

thousands of miles of dangerous wires. At the time, every electric, telephone, and telegraph company put up its own poles and wires, as did the police and fire departments and private burglar-alarm companies. A law passed two years before required that all poles be taken down and the wires placed underground, but absolutely no one had complied with the order. As a result, poles stretched 50 to 150 feet in the air and carried from 100 to 200 wires each.

After seeing the horse die, Mr. Garrigues decided to close the office and head home. He told May that it was too dangerous for her to go out in the storm, and urged her to stay the night at the office. The stove gave off good heat and there was plenty of wood, he pointed out. Remembering the dead horse in the street below, this seemed like sound advice to May.

Everything went well for several hours, but as the light outside began to dim, the solitary nature of May's situation began to bother her. Deepening the gloom was the fact that the gas and electric streetlights were all out. The lines carrying gas to the lamps ran above the ground and had frozen solid. Eventually, the pull of being with her boarding-house friends won out and May prepared to go home.

Going out into the blizzard required careful planning. People who were able to wore two of everything to fight off the cold. Some fashioned homemade snowshoes to help them walk across the snowy terrain, or wore bags over their heads as protection from the stinging blasts of wind and ice. May removed her bustle, pinned up her long skirt so it was above her boot tops, and used a string to tie her hat in place. For added protection, she tied newspapers around her ankles and chest.

A group of Wall Street stockbrokers surveys the tangled mess of telegraph and telephone wires near their offices. (NEW-YORK HISTORICAL SOCIETY)

Outside, May paused a moment before beginning her journey. She was seventy-seven blocks from home and the wind would be in her face most of the way. Then the thought of staying alone in the office came to her again and she stepped out into the storm.

Instantly, her cape whipped up in her face and she was spun around several times. She had just steadied herself when a stout man in a fur coat came up to her and warned, "Your ears are freezing."

Social customs were very conservative in 1888. A woman was not supposed to talk with a man unless she had been properly introduced to him, and not even the blizzard changed this for May. "Let me pass, sir," she demanded as she pushed him aside and hurried along.

Several blocks later, another man grabbed her and steered her into a doorway. She was about to scream for help when he began rubbing her ears. "People don't realize when their ears are being frosted," he said. May touched one of her ears but did not feel anything at all, which frightened her more than the man did.

The man took hold of her cape and arranged it over May's head so that it would cover her ears but still allow her to see. Then he wished her a safe journey and left.

She proceeded, staying on Broadway for as long as possible, mainly because other pedestrians were trudging along that street. If the company gave her a sense of well-being, there were other sights that made her shudder. At one corner, she saw a man clutching the base of a lamppost and overheard a policeman say that he was dead.

Stunned, May forced herself to keep moving. She probably didn't even notice when she entered what was then the city's theater district. Tonight, the usually gaudily lit theaters were dark and the surrounding streets deserted. Only two plays went on that night and neither drew more than a handful of patrons.

Of course, not even a blizzard could stop the great showman, P. T. Barnum. As scheduled, all eighty-six acts of his circus went on at Madison Square Garden, even though the crowd numbered less than 100. As Barnum himself told his audience, "The storm may be a great show, but I still have the greatest show on earth!"

It was at Union Square that May understood just how savage the storm was. Here, the wind was so fierce it bowled over many pedestrians, especially women in their long dresses. To get across the square, walkers held on to one another's shoulders and went single file.

Onward May plodded, past closed-up and darkened department stores such as Arnold Constable and Lord & Taylor. For most stores, Blizzard Monday had been a complete bust. B. Altman rang up one sale, and that was for a single spool of thread. In fact, the only store that did any business to speak of was E. Ridley and Sons. John J. Meisinger had battled his way to the store that morning and set up a crude, handmade

Bars and saloons were packed on Blizzard Monday. Here, an argument has broken out as one customer insists the Blizzard of 1854 was far worse than the one raging outside at that minute. In the background, two men try to stop a drunk patron from foolishly venturing out into the storm. (NEW-YORK HISTORICAL SOCIETY)

sign that announced: WE HAVE SNOW SHOVELS. John sold all 3,000 of his shovels at one dollar a piece, reaping a handsome profit of $1,800. He not only kept his job, but he received a raise as well.

Shopping was the farthest thing from May's mind at that moment. Warmth and shelter were what she craved. New York City had over 10,000 saloons in 1888, and every one of them did a roaring business on Monday. Homeward-bound businessmen stopped in to warm themselves with a glass or two of whiskey, then struggled up the street until they came to another saloon. Naturally, May never even considered stepping into any of these places. Even if she could get over the reek of whiskey, beer, and cigar smoke, a proper young woman never set foot in such an establishment.

There were numerous coffee shops along her route, too, and May thought about stopping for a cup of hot tea. But every coffee shop she approached was jammed with men. Rubbing shoulders with strange men was not something May could do, so she turned into the wind and pushed on.

At Madison Square, the wind again became furious, and May had to walk backward in order to cross it. May continued up Broadway, away from the wealthy homes and shops and into an area of modest brick apartment buildings.

Eighteen blocks later, at 42nd Street, May headed west to Ninth Avenue where she turned and followed the path of the elevated tracks for the remaining five blocks. Exhaustion was beginning to slow her steps and only the thought of her warm room and soft, comfortable bed kept her moving.

When she reached her street another obstacle confronted her. The wind had swept the snow into a giant 10-foot-tall drift on her side of the street so that all of the front steps were completely covered. May paused a few moments, then summoned up one last burst of energy. She hurried across the street and plunged into the drift, slipping, sliding, and virtually swimming up the steps to the boardinghouse door. Fellow boarders had spotted May by this time and rushed to pull her into the house, where her landlady got her to bed and administered the standard cure for chills and exhaustion — a glass of whiskey. May slept for the next sixteen straight hours, but she would return to work on Wednesday. She was right on time, of course.

May had literally walked into the teeth of the storm and survived because of her youthful energy, iron determination, and intelligence. Others weren't so fortunate.

At about the same time that May Morrow set out for home, the Singer Sewing Machine Company in Elizabeth, New Jersey, dismissed its workers for the day. Three young women exited the front gate,

There were restaurants, coffee shops, and saloons for every economic class. In poor neighborhoods and along the waterfront, tiny coffee booths served up hot coffee, cakes, and light meals for just a few pennies. (AUTHOR'S COLLECTION)

joined arms, and set off for the nearby train station. They were instantly assaulted by the wind, battered, and turned around until they lost their way in the whirling white. Their bodies were discovered the next day still within sight of the factory gates.

Meanwhile, James Marshall and his two friends left the same factory by a rear door and hiked to their rowboat. James took the oars and the trio pushed off.

If possible, the wind seemed stronger and the snow heavier than during their morning journey. They couldn't even see the shore of Staten Island, so James aimed the boat as best he could and then struggled to stay on course. Rough waves slapped against the boat, and before long the trio's clothes were soaked through and icing up. James rowed on with the same fierce determination that had gotten May home safely.

At first, his friends encouraged him and bailed water from the boat. But as time crept by, they grew quiet and less animated in the numbing cold. Two hours later, the boat scraped bottom and James leaped out to see where they were. His friends were barely conscious.

He had no way of knowing it at the time, but the boat had come ashore two miles below their normal landing place. What James found when he looked around was a frozen landscape and absolutely no sign of life.

The wind let up for a few seconds, just enough time for James to make out a haystack in a field 600 feet away. One at a time, James dragged his friends to the stack and covered them up with hay to keep them warm. His own clothes were heavy with ice, and fatigue was setting in as well. To keep himself warm, he began trotting around the haystack. Darkness fell and still James kept on racing around and around. To stop, he knew, would almost certainly mean death.

While James was running, another man stepped out into the storm also determined to get home. Roscoe Conkling had spent the day at his law office, so consumed with work that he barely noticed the storm outside his window. When he emerged from the building at 5 P.M. even the usually unflappable former senator was taken aback by the increased power of the blizzard.

As Conkling stood there, a young man named William Sulzer approached him and asked if he wanted to share a cab uptown. Sulzer was a lawyer and thinking about going into politics (he would eventually be elected governor of New York State). He was also a shrewd fellow and knew that a friendship with Conkling might be helpful politically.

Conkling asked Sulzer what such a ride might cost and was shocked by the fifty-dollar fee. "I don't know about you, young man," Conkling grumped, "but I'm strong enough to walk." And without another word, the older man stalked off.

Sulzer tagged after Conkling, still hoping to strike up a conversation. This proved extremely difficult. Conkling was walking very quickly. Besides, both men had to walk with heads bowed to keep snow and bits of street debris out of their eyes. Finally, when they came to a hotel, the younger man gave up and went inside to rent a room.

Conkling did not even break stride to say good-bye, but continued barreling through the snow. "I went magnificently along," Conkling would boast the next day, "shouldering through drifts and headed for the north."

Block after block, Conkling battled wind and snow. Ice collected on his clothes, weighing him down and making each step a chore. It took him two hours to make the two-mile journey from his office to Union Square Park. "I was pretty well exhausted when I got [there], and wiping the snow from my eyes, tried to make out the [path]. But it was im-

Artist Otto Stark has captured the raw power of the storm in this view of pedestrians attempting to cross Union Square. (AUTHOR'S COLLECTION)

possible. There was no light, and I plunged right on in as straight a line as I could."

Halfway across the square, Conkling stopped to rest, holding on to the base of a gaslight for support. It wasn't long before another traveler recognized Conkling and tried to engage him in conversation. The former senator found the man's chatter annoying, so he pushed off from the gaslight and continued plowing ahead. It would take him another hour to go nine blocks to Madison Square. By this time, every step was a struggle and his eyesight was severely limited by the ice caked on his eyebrows and lashes. The next thing Conkling knew, he had stumbled and fallen into a snowdrift up to his neck.

"For nearly twenty minutes I was stuck there and I came as near giving up and sinking down to die as a man can and not do it." Conkling squirmed and flailed until he freed himself. "When I reached the New York Club at 25ᵗʰ Street, I was covered all over with ice and packed snow. . . ."

Conkling collapsed at the door, but attendants at the club saw him and carried him to the hotel where he lived. It was 10 P.M. when Conkling finally pulled the covers up for a much-needed sleep.

The storm, however, did not rest. Its center had only moved a few miles since 3 P.M., and wind speeds of 50, 60, and 70 miles per hour were being recorded in Boston, Provincetown, New Haven, New York City, Eastport, and elsewhere. Temperatures dropped with the disappearance of the sun. Roscoe Conkling did not realize it, but when he left his office at 5 P.M. the temperature stood at 14 degrees Fahrenheit. By the time he collapsed in front of the New York Club, the temperature was at a frigid 8 degrees. For those exposed to the blizzard during the long night, this would be the cruelest time of all.

SIX

RULED BY WIND AND SNOW AND RUIN

Throughout the afternoon and early evening, people made their way home, stumbling through front doors, exhausted and caked in a white glaze. The luckiest were greeted with a warm fire, dry clothes, and a hot meal.

Many others also made it home, but their greetings weren't always so cozy. This was the army of people who made up the working poor — men, women, and children who labored all day but barely earned enough money to survive. Bellhops, bootblacks, sewing machine operators, street sweeps, lamplighters, newspaper boys, messengers, and a host of other unskilled workers were a part of this group, as were the Italians who had spent the day trying to clear the railroad tracks.

The fortunate ones returned to tiny apartments that might house two or three families. Ordinarily, these cramped, airless rooms were intolerable. On Blizzard Monday, the closed-in spaces actually helped the small stoves heat the space more efficiently.

Despite these wretched conditions, there were tens of thousands of people who would have viewed such an apartment as luxurious. Many

For "three cents a spot" a person could get out of the blizzard and maybe even find a dry place on the floor to sleep. (AUTHOR'S COLLECTION)

poor people were living in buildings put up when George Washington was president that were in such bad shape, they were more like unheated sheds.

Writer Charles Edward Russell visited a number of these tenement houses and was appalled by what he found. "The front walls are of brick; the rear and side walls are wooden. On the wooden walls the clapboards sag and sway and are falling off, the ancient laths and plaster are exposed beneath. . . . An icy wind blew through these apertures."

Russell then went through a narrow, gloomy passageway to the backyard, where he found another tenement with seven families inside. After describing the many broken windows and the dank decay of the structure, Russell concluded, "When the building was new and clean, it might have been a tolerable place to house horses. It was never, at any time, a tolerable place in which to house human beings. For fifty or sixty years it has been unfit for anything except burning."

George Steidler was seven and living in such a tenement on Houston Street during the blizzard. "The tenements were malodorous and overrun with rats and vermin," Steidler would write many years later. "At night, one feeble gas jet illuminated the hall off the street and one lit every other floor. They were turned off at 10 P.M., and one had to grope about on the rickety stairs in absolute blackness."

His building had running water "with only one sink in the hall for every four families. Our toilets were 'backhouses' in the yard. . . . During the storm, these were buried in mountains of snow and were inaccessible. With water freezing and pipes bursting, the families dumped garbage or worse in those sinks. Slops ran over when the drains became stuffed and flowed into hallways and down the steps. . . ."

Because there was no refrigeration, perishable items such as meat, poultry, fish, and butter were usually bought on the day they were to be used. Most households had laid in food to last the weekend on the previous Friday. By the end of Blizzard Monday, food supplies were just about exhausted. Steidler's family had only some dry bread, a little cheese, and a plate of cooked cabbage.

Even something as basic as milk was in short supply. "People hung tin pails on their doorknobs and every morning the milkman filled them with a dipper from his bucket. . . . We never knew what we would find floating in our milk." Of course, they found no milk in the pail on Monday morning.

"Coal was purchased from the grocer in five- and ten-cent quantities," Steidler recalled. "During the blizzard we suffered terribly from lack of coal. . . ." The boy and his family wandered around their apartment in three layers of clothes, and resorted to burning what little furniture they had for warmth.

As hard as it is to believe, there were still thousands of people who were in even worse shape than those in the most horrible tenements. A noted charity worker of the time, Helen Campbell, estimated that every day approximately "sixty thousand women and men [spent] the night in the streets of New York City." As for homeless children, Campbell believed around 15,000 of them were without shelter during the blizzard.

Where did they stay on Monday night? Hundreds were able to find a bed or chair at one of the twenty-five privately run charity shelters scattered around the city. Still others spent the night in one of the city's

The mission on Water Street gave each homeless man a sandwich and a cup of hot, black coffee. In return, they had to listen to an hour-long sermon on the wickedness of drinking alcohol. (AUTHOR'S COLLECTION)

thirty-five police precincts, or in soup kitchens or church basements. The all-night restaurants were jammed with people seeking warmth and five-cent platters of pig snouts and cabbage, as were the stale-beer joints and underground lodging cellars where a weary person could purchase a spot on the bench or floor for just three cents.

Many could not even afford the three cents to find shelter. Helen Campbell observed sadly: "It is not till one sees them curled up on doorsteps, tucked away in old barrels and empty packing-boxes, sleeping in coal cellars under the sidewalk, lying in any and every sheltered spot, that one begins to realize that there is no softer pillow for them."

New York City wasn't the only place with a homeless population. Every city, big and small, had its share. In Hoboken, New Jersey, a village of squatters' shacks near the Hudson River was so completely covered over with snow that only a few feeble pinpoints of light could be seen from a nearby road. No one — not the police, not the well-meaning charity workers, and not the reporters searching for a good story — ever bothered to visit these sites during the storm.

One of the saddest things about the storm was that for every horrible story one heard, there was always another even more dreadful. William Inglis spent all of Monday bouncing around the interior of the pilot boat *Colt*. The hurricane winds had whipped the ocean into an endless series of towering waves, some of them 50 to 70 feet high.

As long as the captain kept the boat heading into the waves, everything was fine. The boat would ride up, and up, and up the front face of the wave, until it plowed through the crest. It would then speed down the backside of the wave until it reached the bottom or trough, where the next wave would begin lifting it up again. Hundreds of times this happened, over and over again. Up and up, then down and down, with the captain ever on the alert for a shift in the direction of the waves. As night came, the storm's fury never slackened for a moment.

All of the pilots had come below, as had most of the crew, and everyone sat around the cabin riding out the storm. Few words were spoken, and time passed slowly in this tense way. Then, just as Inglis felt himself giving in to sleep, "a big sea hit the poor schooner solidly . . . and lifted her upward and backward as a hard punch in the jaw will lift a man. . . . A second great wave hit her in the side, and over she went on her beam ends. Everything not tied in place came banging down. Down lay the poor schooner like a horse shot in battle."

A great green torrent of water burst through the main hatch, while another poured into the aft companionway. "The twin floods met and frothed as they chafed at each other. [The] hard-coal fire in the cabin stove . . . sent up a cloud of steam and gas when the water struck it so that it was impossible to see in the cabin."

Men were tossed from bunks and chairs, landing on top of one another or slamming into beams and floating furniture. Inglis had grabbed hold of a railing and hung "pendulum fashion, out of my berth to windward, or rather skyward, my elbows on either side keeping me from tumbling down and my legs waving to and fro helplessly."

The next moment, the schooner began to move. "She rose like a human being, fighting with the awful waves and righted herself as nimbly as a boxer jumps away from a blow. The whole crew was on deck by this time. . . . They began to work the pumps fore and aft and lightened her all they could."

Even hanging upside down, Inglis was impressed with how quickly the men recovered from the tremendous shock and how coolly they were working to save the boat.

"I would like to say a word here, too, for Manuel Gomez, our stew-

A stern-to-bow view of a large sailing vessel encased in ice (Delaware Public Archives)

ard. He had just finished cooking dinner when the schooner, falling down, sent everything flying. . . . With almost certain death at his heels, that man calmly stood in the galley and fished around for his flying and floating pots and saucepans. He swore at the wave . . . and called it bad names in good Portuguese swear-words. Then, seeing me hanging disconsolate by the elbows in the cabin, with woe written all over my sea-sick face, he came in and tried to cheer me up by calling the wave more choice names. . . ."

With the steward's help, Inglis got his feet planted on the floor of the cabin. "Outside it was dark . . . and in the cabin the single swinging lamp showed destruction written everywhere. All the berths . . . were flooded. The fair white and gold ceiling was blackened and dented where flying hot coals and cinders had struck it. The carpets and rugs were all washing around. . . .

"The hurricane was still howling, and vast waves thumped and shook our boat again and again as they tried to throw her. Four times in ten minutes it seemed to me she was on her beam ends once more, but she righted herself each time. . . . I had often heard about vessels being on their beam ends but I had never comprehended it. It means death. . . ."

Later, one of the pilots came into the cabin and a shaken Inglis tried to find out how bad their situation really was. "Said I to [him], 'Will you bet 5 to 8 that we come out of this all right?' Said he, 'My lad, we must put our trust in Providence. . . .'"

Over on the mainland, the bitter cold, icy winds, and stinging snow swept across a darkened and abandoned landscape. Those in rural areas had long ago secured any doors or gates that might be swept away by a powerful gust, and gotten animals fed and attended to for the night. Emergency journeys outdoors were accomplished at the end of a strong rope tied to a stair rail.

Cities big and small seemed empty of life as well. Historian Irving

Newspapers rushed out special editions on the blizzard. This "Icicle Edition" by the New York Morning Journal *featured stranded commuters, a newsboy hero who continued selling papers throughout the storm, and a feature on "Panic in Mid-Air" ("mid-air" being on the elevated railroad tracks).* (NEW-YORK HISTORICAL SOCIETY)

SPECIAL **SNOW** SHEET.

Morning Journal.

ICICLE EDITION.

NO. 1,926.

NEW YORK, TUESDAY, MARCH 13, 1888.

PRICE ONE CENT.

BLIZZARD EXTRA

THE SNOW TERROR.

New York Tied Up and Cut Off by Storm.

PARALYZED CITIES.

Cars, Trains, Business, Theatres Stopped.

ACCIDENTS, MISHAPS.

Graphic Pictures of the Worst Day in Fifty Years by the Journal's Hardy Staff.

A storm which struck New York a few hours after midnight yesterday and has raged with intermission until the hour of going to press the severest that has visited the city in years. The rain of Sunday night turned to snow, the wind rose to a tremendous fury and the temperature fell to 10 above zero.

At 2 A. M. eight inches of snow had fallen.

At 10 A. M. eighteen inches had covered the level.

At 6 o'clock there were three feet of snow on the level.

The storm extended over all Long Island, New York State, New Jersey, Pennsylvania, nearly as far South as Pittsburg and over the State of...

The wind was from the northwest and averaged forty miles an hour.

The temperature fell to 5 degrees above zero.

At 10 o'clock all travel on the Elevated roads was suspended on the four lines in New York, though the Second Avenue line resumed for a time in the evening. The Third Avenue resumed at intervals near midnight. All expect to run to-day.

Over a million people were kept from their occupations.

On the exchanges, all the courts but two, some of the mercantile houses, all the shipping houses closed or did no business.

But four of the theatres were closed.

Not at those who reached their business houses nor downtown sought hotels or lodging for the night.

All these were packed last night.

Less on the principal avenues little was done than on the sidewalks, hence walking was next to impossible.

No mails were received yesterday; none sent out of the city. No ships or steamers arrived or sailed.

The railroad lines out of the city were closed. Telegraph wires were broken everywhere and communication almost completely cut off. The last wire out of the city gave out at...

The blizzard beleaguerment of New York was complete.

Staten Island was isolated and Coney Island severely damaged by the storm.

A serious accident occurred on the Elevated...

Minor mishaps or hundreds are reported.

It is feared that during the night many people may have lost their lives in the snowdrifted streets uptown.

The storm is expected to last another twenty hours. At midnight the wind was howling as fiercely as ever.

ANCIENT RESIDENTS AMAZED.

A Visitation That Surpassed Anything in This Generation.

...

with the snow and wind, he was disconcerted at not finding his usual carriage running along.

All the street-cars were stopped.

When all the horse-cars stop, New York is very near a revolution. But the citizen spoke of it as a thing further and found not only a revolution, but an earthquake.

He walked along—as means of riding being at hand—to an Elevated Railroad station and boarded a train to go "downtown."

Then he learned what a blizzard was.

The Elevated trains wouldn't run.

New York had been struck by the most terrible, the most measureable storm it has had for more than half a century, perhaps the most violent storms that ever came here, but the big, red service clerk yet old enough to remember, and nobody else has authority to speak.

Then the average citizen tried to get a cab.

There were cabs running up and down town. People who were unable to breast the storm and walk to business were unable to get to their homes and offices.

A Good Day for Cabbies.

But it cost them a good bit. A Ransom cab from Forty-second street to the Sub-Treasury building cost $10 before 12 o'clock, noon. By the middle of the afternoon it cost $25.

A Journal reporter offered a hackman $20 to take him from Cushman square to the scene of the accident, seventy-sixth street, and was laughed to scorn.

Newspaper Row Beats the Deck.

Nowhere else in New York did the blizzard spend itself as it did around Newspaper Row. The cluster of tall buildings that catch the breeze from the upper parts of the atmosphere and send it swirling down through the streets made whirlwinds more a difficulty and then an impossibility about the lower end of Park row.

In spots the earth was blown bare. The car-tracks made levers of the high wind and the high buildings had scooped the earth bare—but only in spots. In those spots the wind was enough to catch the weary pedestrian by his heels and send him sprawling on the small of his back.

All the Streets Impassable.

All over town the streets were choked up. Commissioner Coleman's promise of clean streets for the rest of the year was among the things of the past.

All the loose, dangling things, such as awnings and signs, went flying...

WASHINGTON ON WALL STREET.

...

ELEVATED TRAVEL STOPPED.

Angry Crowds at the Scene—Passengers in Deadly Peril.

The New Yorkers who first realized that a wild Western blizzard, with the short of the prairie and the howl of the mountain wolf, had struck this town were those who got up about 6 o'clock in the morning and ploughed their way to the Elevated stations. They found train sleds leading to the station platforms a troublesome slide, the snow so completely covering them that the stops were indistinguishable.

These who managed to get upstairs, however, were a little surprised to find the station crowded with men, women and children, some fuming and fretting, others laughing and joking and not a few men letting off some tall-size words which were quite in keeping with their Western surroundings. Tan poor ticket-seller had a hard time of it. When he told people that the chances for getting downtown that morning by the Elevated were very slim, they turned on him and roared to know what kind of a road it was, anyway.

"If ain't my fault, sir, the blizzard is to blame."

No Trains for Hours.

Never had travel on the Elevated been so completely blocked as yesterday. At the opening of the day's business the trains ran at intervals of about twenty-five minutes, and as the day advanced they grew fewer and further between, and at times they were more apart.

On the Ninth avenue line all the stations down as far as Desbrosses street were packed with people all anxious to reach their respective places of business. Not only were the waiting-rooms crowded, but the platforms outside enriched masses of humanity of all sizes, sizes and both sexes, huddled together and shivering like sheep.

Some waited for an hour or so and then left in disgust; others waited over 5 hour, growing up and down the track before having examining the conditions of the road before starting a hopeful shower of the boy head but swallowed up their free-cigil tickets, and suddenly away easily to the street, where they stood in a dilemma as to what course to pursue. There were no surface cars running, and to go down-town was a clear case of potsherding the old reliable ways of Mr. Shanks.

Tickets Taken All the Same.

There was considerable grumbling among the anxious crowds about the action of the Elevated people in taking their money and keeping it after it was found that no return could be given.

This matter was the cause of frequent boisterous altercations with the ticket-sellers. But they were unavoidable. The ticket-sellers might freely have it to his chest and putting of the angry people, conspicuously tell them quiet, rage and sweat.

From 7 o'clock onward it was almost impossible to board a train when it did arrive. It was the same on all the lines. When the train reached the stations the car platforms were so densely packed with people that unless a passenger wanted to get off the gates were not opened, and then it was impossible to get on or off.

Drivers Waded Knee Deep in Snow.

Even in this bitter weather the walk from Grand street to Harlem is a brisk walk few would care to embrace. But though the blinding drift of gnawing and the violent hurricane through most of the foot of snow was a hardship which New Yorkers had never before been called upon to experience.

Hundreds of women who undertook the journey were overcome before it was half accomplished and sank exhausted in the snow, whence they would have died but for kind hands carried them to places of safety. Strong men also were prostrated, as the station-house records to-day...

...

preferred it to remaining, for they knew not how long in the crowded train.

Several times when the track ahead was full of pedestrian trains started, causing a panic among the imperilled people. But so far as learned no fatalities resulted from these occurrences.

As the snow hour approached and the severity of the storm rather increased than diminished the trains ran more slowly and were dispatched less frequently.

The Great Danger.

The snow packed so hard in between the two guard rails that ran beside the iron rails that the engineers feared to run their trains.

The danger was that the wheels of the engine, perhaps of the cars, would run up on the snow. Then a train might topple over into the street. This is the one accident most dreaded by the Manhattan Company.

The Ladders from the Elevated.

A three-car train on Sixth avenue going down town was stopped at 8:30 a. m. in Third street, between Sixth avenue and South Fifth avenue.

And not only did it come to a stop, but it stayed stationary so long that there was scant hope among the passengers of any release till the storm should blow over.

Presently the Fire Department was called upon, and the nearest hook and ladder company coming to the rescue, planted ladders against the Elevated road structure.

Before that some of the younger passengers had managed to wait half to the Eighth street station. By some miracle they were not blown off the track and returned to the train, glad enough to get away from the cutting wind.

When the ladders were put in position the younger and more adventurous of the passengers started to escape from the train to the street. Few of the ladies in the trains were venturesome enough to trust themselves to the ladders at first, but as the hours went by they became...

Snarled in Telegraph Wires on Broadway.

...bolder, and at last, rendered desperate by the cold, their fear to the winds and wrapping their skirts tightly about them, surrendered themselves to the tender mercies of the ladder monopoly and reached terra firma in safety.

The wind and the snow, however, so confused them that half a dozen, one after the other, of them went tumbling to the street, and the firemen, fearing disaster, promptly took away their ladders.

Then a bridge was built from the train as it stood, blocked on the road, to the windows of the people shop of the 27th Department. It was made of planks with a ladder on either side for a guard rail.

Over this bridge the passengers clambered and, making their escape to the "rescue safety of the streets" went backward or forward till business as their labor dictated.

For the first two hours that we were imprisoned there," said a passenger, "we were unable to speak a civil word. Then after that everybody seemed to grow reconciled and began to see fun in the situation and to enjoy it. After that there was lots of fun."

It was so nice on the Elevated road on the East side. The reporter, in company with more than a hundred other unfortunate, stood on a second avenue station after it was known that the Third, Sixth and Ninth avenue Roads were all blocked, and the people were peculiar in spite of the storm that pelted them.

An engine came along and was cheered. Then it was seen that there was no train behind the engine.

"Had ease to that engineer," said one burly looking fellow. "What for would he come without a train?"

On the Sixth avenue Road the last train down reached Franklin street at 10:30. On the other lines traffic ceased entirely at about 12:30. It was resumed an hour afterward, however, on the Second avenue line only. But trains there only ran once as far as Grand and Allen streets. From that time on the Elevated, though the Sixth street was the only point at which trains could be taken for uptown. It was, in fact, the grand central station for travel to the city.

When the vast crowds of people on their way home in the evening had climbed up the icy stairways they were met with the startling announcement, printed in big chalk letters:

Upon inquiry at the ticket office the people were informed that a few trains were running on the Second Avenue line from the Grand street station. To those who lived in the upper part of the city this was welcome information, and there was a grand rush from all parts of the town for the route of Grand and Allen streets.

Those who lived below Fiftieth streets had to walk home. To this they shoved their good judgment.

By 5 o'clock for blocks in the vicinity of Grand and Allen the streets were jammed with people. Everybody who thought it was possible to ride uptown had gone to that point. As a consequence it was soon apparent to all that at the rate the trains were running the innovation would soon could not be carried to their destinations in a few weeks.

Thousands, therefore, were obliged to queue in the inevitable and walk home. This was an undertaking which appalled even the most robust men and seemed impossible for the women and young girls.

Did High Prices for a Ride.

For the hackman the blizzard proved a veritable bonanza. Carriages, cars, hacks, wagons, vehicles of every sort were in demand everywhere. The hackmen made their own bargains and the charges were refined to abide by them. Black eyes and broken ribs naturally enough suited. In Union square the hackmen practiced a systematic union gleam.

They would guarantee to land passengers almost any where they liked for $1, and to bring their money in advance and after travelling a few blocks declare that the snow was too much for them, or that their horses were exhausted and refuse to drive a foot further. Parties of working girls who had subscribed $2 or $3 for a fare were frequently turned out by a half-drunken hackman in some deserted street and left them shivering in three feet of snow.

A HORSE-CAR WATERLOO.

Double and Triple Teams Unable to Move the Cars.

For the first time in sixteen years New York experienced a universal suspension of street traffic. On every car of every car-line there was a tie-up, while cabs, wagons, hacks and all manner of vehicles were sooner or later stranded in the snow.

Before daylight every line was running the cars and every car started on time. Few, however, reached City Hall. Most of them were abandoned en route, and even the snow-ploughs, with...

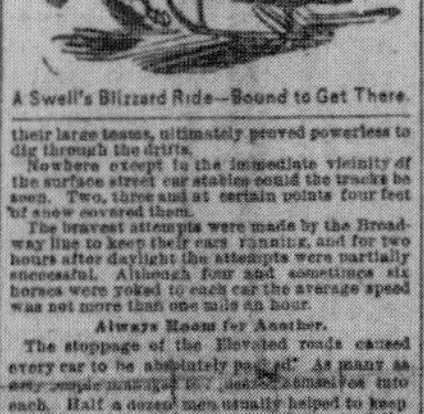

"Stalled" on Third Avenue.

...der $25. Ten dollars to ride down town was a common hack fare.

Suffering Among the Drivers.

The Third Avenue drivers had a very hard time of it. Turning up one or two at the depot they walked into the main office, and those in charge, as long as eggs hanging in their beards. Every man had a tale of suffering.

"I thought I had a team of horses that could pull anything," continued a sturdy driver, "but I don't think so any more."

At 9:30 a. m. Superintendent Robinson issued general orders to withdraw all the cars from the tracks. By noon the order was complied with from the Battery to Harlem, but half a dozen cars between City Hall and the depot were abandoned on the road.

Always Room for Another.

The stoppage of the Elevated roads caused every car to be absolutely pack'd as soon as any appeared on any of the ground routes for such. Half a dozen men usually helped to keep the driver warm, twice as many hung on at the...

"HELLO CENTRAL, HELLO!"

Communication by Telegraph and Telephone Almost Entirely Cut Off.

The lot of the telegraph operator was not a happy one yesterday. He or she, as the case may be, who was acquainted...

...click" for innumerable repetitions, and even then the message was generally disconnected and sometimes indivisible.

The great operating room on the sixth floor of the Western Union building, which usually is sounds with the merry click of the instruments, was shrouded with an oppressive silence, only broken occasionally. Almost 75 per cent of the instruments were unattended by their operators.

Communication Cut Off.

Chief Operator Brainard, when questioned about the condition of the wires said:

"We are completely cut off from Philadelphia, Baltimore, Washington, Norfolk and Richmond, Trenton, Paterson, and in fact every place along the seaboard. Our wires are all down, and communication with the South is out of the question."

"We have three wires to Buffalo and Cleveland and are able to connect with Chicago, Cincinnati, St. Louis and the West and northwest in this way. Our offices all over the country have been instructed to send messages by transmission on the understanding the send messages will be sent, subject to delays at all points.

"The storm is as far as we can learn does not extend..."

A Windy Corner Near the Brooklyn Bridge.

...tall with the conductor and an occasional small boy was to be seen perched on the roof.

At 9 o'clock the Broadway line had to be abandoned. The great cross-town lines whose places in Union square, all along the route fixed cabs were standing in drifts. The drivers invariably took their horses to the nearest stables.

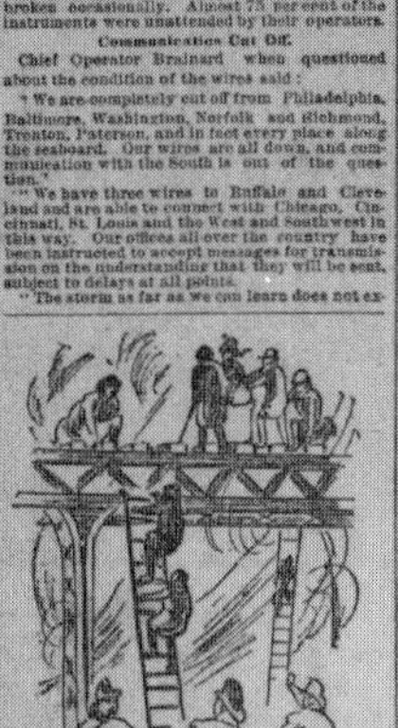

The first car on the Third Avenue line left One Hundred and Twenty-sixth street at 4:30 a. m. It reached the Post Office at 9 o'clock. The last to arrive downtown left the One Hundred and Twenty-sixth street station at slow. It was crewed with workmen and working women and got as far as Park place by 6 o'clock. Speaking of this journey to a Journal reporter, Conductor Conway H. Post said it was the jolliest he ever piloted.

On leaving Harlem all the passengers were strangers to him and to one another. By the time Park place was reached everyone knew everyone else and had contracted such friendship that the parting was indeed most sorrowful.

Only three other cars succeeded in covering the entire route.

Several cars ran adrift between One Hundred and sixth and Eighty-sixth streets. More than managed to get down as far as Sixty-seventh street after six o'clock were stalled in the company's stables.

Cars Stalled in the Snow.

There was hardly a true less almost as unfortunate as the Eighth, which did not get a single car to its destination downtown. At intervals of a mile along Fourth and Madison avenues up to Eighty-fourth street stalled-up cars were to be seen. One driver did land passengers opposite the Astor House, but he had the assistance of six horses. The hardest snow-pinch of the line was started out at half-past 8, not the rising gale carried the snow a foot deep on the tracks as quickly as the plough cleared it away. After half an hour a work the team was given up for the day.

Little success rewarded indefatigable efforts on the part of the management of the Sixth Avenue line. In spite of a magnificent snow-plough and six horses to every car only three drivers succeeded even reached.

The Sixth line ran fairly well between 5 and 7 o'clock, but the force wind that swept in from the river piled the drifts so high as to halt progress after 7:15 an impossibility. The Belt-versity place also stopped running at 6:30, and those on the Seventh avenue exactly one hour later.

The Avenue B bobtails were uncommonly fortunate. Six of them crossed the Post Office. Not one of the Avenue C lines landed passengers below Bleecker.

Fire in a Snow-storm.

...

ALL WIRES ARE DOWN.

At 12 O'Clock a Complete Telegraphic Interruption is Announced.

At 12 o'clock last night the United Press sent out the following:

Since 7 p. m. we have had for part of the time communication with points in New York State and West to Chicago, but we are now again cut off from all points. The wire we had was the only one working West out of New York. It was one of the old Baltimore & Ohio wires. It is now broken between Weehawken and Haverstraw, as well as all others by that route. The Western Union have no wires, nor the Postal. We have not any Eastern point, nor Philadelphia, Baltimore nor Washington, nor to-night.

FLAMES FANNED BY WIND.

Firemen Struggle Amid Snowdrifts Short of Feet—A Memorial Night Panic.

The holdout firemen felt a chill of fear when a sudden alarm rang out from the box at Canal and Varick streets at 7:15 last night. It had been preceded twenty minutes before by a first alarm from the box at Canal and West Broadway.

As the engines turned out the snow-clouds were already glowing with the ruddy reflection of the flames. No one doubted that a disastrous conflagration was at hand. The alarm's terrible smoke with "4" drifts the first two engines reached the scene the big four-story brick factory No. 9 and 11 Laight street was found to be blazing from cellar to roof.

Fanned by the breath of the blizzard, the flames went through its old air, scattering huge...

Blizzard or No Blizzard the Little Hero Was There.

...brands down the wind and threatening destruction to the whole block. It was then that the second call was sent from box No. 208, at Varick street, followed instantly by a special call for Engine No. 33, in Great Jones street, in all summoning eight engines and four truck.

At the expiration of half an hour ten fire engines had succeeded in getting the conflagration to some dangerous. Engines Nos. 20 and 21 had work fast to get the water back to the house and stayed out the several stories of the company. Engines Nos. 13 and 27 stuck fast in drifts and it was not until 27 and managed to proceed after additional horses had been pressed into its services.

Lines were run through the Hygeanic Hotel, separated from the burning building by narrow alleyway, and the firemen drove to the upper stories. They accomplished little for the furious blast which swept the alley except the solid stream as will and entered them in driving mist. In Varick street, immediately in the rear of the fire, the hundreds of Italians huddled in a row of tenement houses fled in dismay.

In an hour all was over; the fire had burned itself out. All told remained of the factory were four tottering walls which soon afterward went down below the zero. The buildings were occupied by Messers. Freedman & Co., paper box manufactured, on the upper floors, and George Curtis, stationer, on the ground floor, was completely cleared out an amount of $50,000.

After the fire was over Messrs. Paterson & Silvey procured a draft of twenty-five horses from Harlem and organized mounted brigade of twenty-five men who patrolled the dry-goods district during the rest of the night.

THE BLIZZARD'S VICTIMS.

Accidents By the Storm in Every Section of the City.

At Police Headquarters the gravest anxiety was depicted on the faces of all the officials. With the failure of almost the entire telegraphic system of the department the Central Office was completely isolated, leaving the commanding officers in painful ignorance of what was occurring.

After something an alarm officers were ordered to proceed with all speed to the nearest fire quarters and turn out the engines. Line men were sent out to try to repair the damage, but their feeble efforts were fruitless from The men and the snow and they were soon forced to desist.

Electric Alarm Kept Up.

Renewed anxiety was felt at the Central Office when early in the afternoon a notification came from the electric light companies that they were no longer able to operate their plant, and that in consequence of the principal thoroughfares would be in darkness. Special officers were at once detailed on the station-houses and all in p. m. reduced the men were notified to exercise extraordinary vigilance.

Detectives Fink and Luthiar on their way to Jefferson Market were caught at Eleventh street and...

PANIC IN MID-A...

A Fatal Collision on the ... Avenue Elevated.

SNOW BLINDS THE ENGINE

One Man Killed and Several Serious Injuries.

A heavily-loaded train pulled by ... was slowly puffing southward over the packed tracks of the Third Avenue "L." at 7 o'clock yesterday morning.

As the train reached the Seventy-... station the waiting crowds on ... jostled each other in a mad ... foothold on the car platforms, large ... in ...

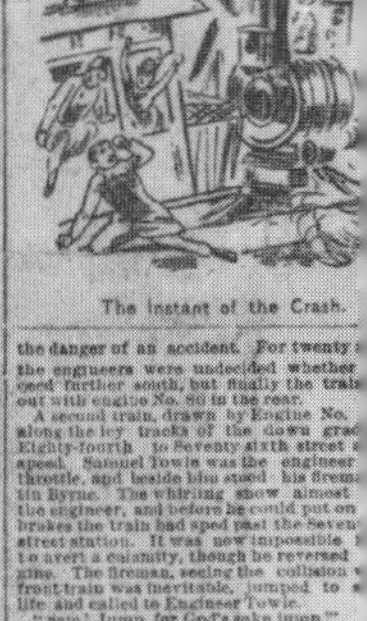

The Instant of the Crash.

...danger of an accident. For twenty ... the engineers were undecided whether ... good further south, but finally the train ... out with engine No. 80 in the lead.

A second train, drawn by Engine No. ... along the icy tracks of the down-grade ... Eighty-fourth to Seventy-sixth street ... appeal. Samuel Towle was the engineer ... train No. 80. The whirling snow almost ... the engineer, and before he could put on ... brakes the train had sped past the Seventy-... street station. It was imperceptible ... to avert a calamity, though he reversed ... gine. The fireman, seeing the collision ... front train was inevitable, jumped to ... life and called to Engineer Towle.

"Save! Jump, for God's sake jump!"

But the engineer remained at his post ... for his life. In a moment engine No. ... dashed into engine No. 80. As the two ... rebounded from the mighty set-to, engi ... crouched into the first two engines of ... reached the scene the big four-story ... tory No. 9 and 11 Laight street was found ... blazing from cellar to roof.

...

A great number of the passengers w ... ed at first but it proved hard to extri ... them from no snow-drift. Rumors that ... an fifty people were killed passed from ... other, but the following list tells the ... comers to life and limb:

...

Cold and Snow To-day.

The temperature at Hudnut's pharmacy ... day was 28 degrees above zero. At 6 ... ground it as 19 degrees at 9 a. m. For ... the ground was 19 degrees at 9 a. m. ... below zero. The wire-tied engineer ... slightly cold to all the station-houses, and ... p. m. reduced the men were notified ...

The weather for to-day will be cold an ... weather. It will be preceded by a ... probably reach 20 above zero. The wind ... high water on Sandy Hook at 8:1 and ... day. There will not be very much ...

Werstein described Manhattan as "practically a ghost town, its streets and avenues ruled by wind and snow and ruin; vehicles of all sorts lay overturned in the roadways. Some teamsters had unhitched their horses and led them to safety in nearby livery stables, but others had simply left both vehicles and animals where they stood, bogged down in the snow. The corpses of frozen horses poked stiff-legged out of snow-drifts; abandoned horsecars stood in long rows on cross streets; shattered store signs hung askew; uprooted trees lay in parks and squares."

There was still some activity, of course. Policemen plunged out into the cold to walk their beats, not to deter crime, but to pull hapless drunks from snowdrifts. Firemen remained on duty, though virtually every alarm box in New York City was useless because of downed wires. Fortunately, only two large blazes broke out during the entire blizzard, and these were brought under control before they were able to spread.

Indoors, Sergeant Francis Long and the rest of the weather station crew stayed past quitting time to monitor the storm. And at least one other business was fighting to stay open as well — the newspapers.

Newspaper editors and reporters had woken on Monday to find themselves surrounded by the biggest story of the year. Those who made it to their offices that morning were immediately sent out to interview politicians and prominent businessmen. Artists rushed to draw some of the scenes they had witnessed on the streets.

Now, as Monday evening was drawing to a close, texts were being hastily edited and set in type for Tuesday's early editions. In truth, the newspapers had very little information about the extent of the storm or what was happening in other areas. Just about every telegraph line was down, and even the most energetic reporter couldn't travel very far to see what was really going on. A reporter might talk with the mayor or

Firemen and horses strain to haul this fire engine to a blaze. (AUTHOR'S COLLECTION)

some other town official, but these people really didn't have many additional facts, either. Everyone everywhere was cut off.

To make up for the lack of real information, newspapers used oversized headlines to fill up space. One Philadelphia paper opened with a headline anyone near a window could see for themselves: STORM STILL RAGING.

In New York, the *Sun* covered just about its entire front page with a series of bold headlines:

THE BURIED CITY
New York's Dreadful Sepulture
Under Masses of Snow.

A NIGHT OF DEVASTATION
How the Tempest Howled and Raged
Through the Dark Wilderness of Streets.

PERISHING MEN AND WOMEN
Wanderers Found Dead in Snowdrifts.

AND THE TEMPERATURES BELOW ZERO.

The stories that followed were all very melodramatic in tone and contained few solid details.

Newspapers were so desperate for stories that they often took any rumor that came their way and reported it as fact. The Albany *Times* had one headline scream: STAMFORD DESTROYED, TERRIBLE DISASTER TO A THRIVING CONNECTICUT TOWN. The very brief story that followed pointed out how isolated all towns and cities had become: "The village of Stamford, Connecticut, as reported by a special dispatch, was totally destroyed by fire early this morning. Wires are down and particulars are not obtainable." The report proved to be false; the fire in Stamford had actually been confined to the telegraph office of the local train station.

A few papers tried to maintain a calm tone and report on the storm without resorting to rumors or overly dramatic writing. A Vermont paper, the Bellows Falls *Times*, probably produced the most succinct and yet accurate blizzard story of all: "No paths, no streets, no sidewalks, no light, no roads, no guests, no calls, no teams, no hacks, no trains, no moon, no meat, no milk, no paper, no mails, no news, no thing — but snow."

As Monday drew to a close, the most important event was taking place without anyone being aware of it. Throughout the day, the center of the blizzard had traveled north just off the coast. It was an especially slow-moving storm, which meant it became an incredible blizzard machine — picking up moisture from the ocean, freezing it into snow, and then dumping it onto land.

At 10 P.M. Monday night, the storm center finally touched Massachusetts and then did something that would surprise everyone and add fuel to the notion that the blizzard had an evil mind of its own. The storm turned west and then south, in effect turning around and heading down the coast. It was coming back for a second shot at the already buried eastern states.

S E V E N

WHAT WILL MY POOR CHILDREN DO?

Most people went to bed Monday night assuming the storm would be gone by morning. But when they woke on Tuesday, March 13, they found the white hurricane ruling the outdoors as savagely as ever.

If nothing else, Monday had taught everyone at least one valuable lesson: If you did not absolutely have to go outside you should stay snug and safe indoors. Yet tens of thousands still braved the freezing temperatures and driving snow on Tuesday morning.

Farmers still had to tend to livestock and make hasty repairs to barns and other structures damaged by the wind. Those with essential jobs — such as police and firemen and telegraph wire repairmen — fought their way through snow and around abandoned carriages to do their jobs. And many fearful workers — especially those who had stayed home on Monday — once again donned layers of clothes and set out for work.

Tuesday was also another day of work for the nation's newest immigrants. Railroads had hired the largest number of laborers on Blizzard Monday. On Tuesday, telephone and telegraph offices decided to begin uncovering downed poles and wires, while ferryboat operators hoped

On March 13, the center of the southern storm had turned and was battering Long Island for a second time.

to clear their stations and landing docks. Police and fire departments as well as hospitals sought access to their buildings.

Attitudes concerning snow removal were very different in the nineteenth century. In general, city governments either did not see the removal of snow from the streets as a priority or they did not consider it their responsibility at all. Those cities that did remove snow usually waited until the storm had completely stopped to begin shoveling. Because they did not have large, permanent work crews, they would then have to assemble teams of shovelers and rent the necessary equipment. The most important business areas and the streets where the wealthiest people lived were cleared first. It usually took so long to move snow that most secondary streets melted clean long before the shovelers got around to them.

Other cities felt that it was up to the owners of homes, apartment buildings, and businesses to remove snow from the sidewalks and streets directly in front of their property. These cities passed statutes

Snow removal was a hard and time-consuming job. Here, day laborers shovel snow into wagons, after which it will be taken to the river and dumped. (AUTHOR'S COLLECTION)

requiring such snow removal. A sizable number of citizens felt these laws were unfair and continually challenged them in court from 1833 through the 1920s.

Almost all such laws were eventually upheld in state supreme courts, but this did not mean that citizens fell in line immediately. A substantial number of people simply refused to shovel snow, preferring to let nature take its course.

But the Great Blizzard did change the way a lot of people viewed snow removal. New York City's Superintendent of Streets and Roads, Jacob Coleman, was one of the first to appreciate the change.

Since noon the previous day, Coleman had been receiving frantic messages from Mayor Hewitt and various department heads telling him that a citywide crisis was at hand. Fire equipment couldn't get through; the police were having a hard time patrolling the neighborhoods; food and coal were running low, but delivery wagons couldn't get through. The city was paralyzed and Coleman could sense that his job was on the line unless he could reopen the streets.

Coleman began assembling and sending out his workers long before dawn on Tuesday. By 7 A.M. he had several thousand Italian laborers clearing snow from the Battery north to Union Square. The word *clear* had many meanings that day. In some places, they really did clear the streets of snow — patiently loading it into wagons and hauling it to the river to be dumped.

A boy has conquered this massive pile of snow and now has an unusual view of his town's main street in West Southington, Connecticut. (BARNES MUSEUM)

A resident of Northampton, Massachusetts, surveys the town's main street from the entrance to a snow tunnel. (NEW-YORK HISTORICAL SOCIETY)

Coleman, however, ran into problems immediately. He only had a few dozen wagons at his disposal; to do the job correctly, he estimated that he would need at least 1,000 wagons, and he knew it would take him days to assemble this large a number. Since he wanted to show quick results, Coleman did the only thing he could. He had his shovelers simply toss snow to the side of the street. When they came to hard-packed snow or ice, they merely leveled off the top and pressed on with their work.

This approach saved time, and his crews were able to clear an 11-block stretch of Bowery Street in three hours. The street remained little used at first, because the shovelers had tossed up a solid 10-foot-high wall of snow on both sides of the avenue with no entrances! This didn't bother Coleman in the least. As far as the superintendent was concerned, he had cleared the streets and now it was up to citizens to get to it.

Eventually, people would dig snow tunnels through the mounds and begin to wander along the street. By afternoon, the tunnels were enlarged and horse-drawn sleighs were moving briskly up and down the Bowery with bells tinkling merrily. One resident described the scene as reminiscent of St. Petersburg, Russia. "Of course," she added, "it was most strange to see sleighs at the level of second-floor windows."

During the day, Coleman did some hasty calculations that told him exactly how daunting a job lay ahead. He estimated that over 24 million cubic yards of snow would have to be moved in order to get traffic flowing again. With this information in hand, the city government authorized the hiring of 17,000 laborers at twenty-five cents an hour. Despite the huge number of men, it would be many days before even the most important business and residential streets were passable.

The services of shovelers came under even sharper demand at mid-morning when the snow suddenly lessened. The wind was blowing as hard as before, but people took the lighter snowfall as a sign that the storm was ending and began emerging from their homes. Stores, markets, apartment buildings, hotels, and front stoops all needed clearing and people were happy to pay someone else to do the backbreaking job.

By late morning, the going rate for a shoveler had risen to three dollars a day, and by afternoon, many were commanding and getting four dollars. It wasn't unusual for a worker to quit a job in the middle to take on a higher paying one just down the block.

This produced grumbling about the "unreliable, greedy Italians." Of course, none of the shovelers had contracts to bind them to a job or to guarantee their employment or wages once the emergency was over. In truth, they were doing what any good American businessman would do — watching the market carefully and trying to maximize profits whenever possible.

A second group of shoveling entrepreneurs also appeared, especially in big cities — gangs of boys armed with shovels, brooms, and ice choppers. The charge for clearing a stoop and short stretch of sidewalk ranged from five dollars all the way up to an astronomical twenty-five dollars. Residents were often more than willing to pay the fee to avoid battling the tons of ice and snow at their doorsteps.

People were often astonished by the strange shapes in their yards and neighborhoods that the drifting snow had created. A Massachusetts farmer was amazed to see a drift rising up over the roof of his barn like some giant ocean wave.

An endless line of day laborers struggles to open this road in South Norwalk, Connecticut. (New-York Historical Society)

In New York City and Brooklyn, the early-morning commuters were shocked when they saw the East River. It looked like a solid sheet of ice.

People immediately rushed to the riverbanks and began to speculate on how thick the ice might be and whether it was safe to walk on. Up close, the distance across looked immense and the ice was clearly not a single sheet, but many big and small ice floes jammed together. No one rushed to be first on the ice.

It was then that a Brooklyn boy of eighteen lowered a ladder onto the ice. Cautiously, he climbed down, then proceeded to jump up and down several times. As he came back toward his ladder, he announced that "She's safe as the United States Mint!"

Instantly, many onlookers announced that they wanted to cross the ice bridge. On the Brooklyn side, the boy gladly held his ladder as one hardy soul after another came down, though he made it clear that the fee to use his ladder would be five cents.

"His pockets bulged with coins," one observer noted. "Soon a long file of pedestrians surely numbering at least two hundred were slowly edging toward the Manhattan shore." Similar business operations were set up on the Manhattan side, and in no time at all, the ice swarmed with people.

Another group of ice-crossers also appeared. The unnamed observer recalled that "all the dogs in Brooklyn . . . came barking and bounding onto the [ice] field as well. The pooches were of all sizes, shapes and varieties. . . . Perhaps they, too, had sensed the drama and historic import of the occasion."

More than just men and dogs crossed the ice bridge. Several women were spotted making the journey, while hordes of boys slid down the icy

The first brave individuals venture onto the ice bridge that linked Brooklyn and New York City. (AUTHOR'S COLLECTION)

pilings and raced across the expanse. And at least one horse was hoisted over the side in a sling-harness and ridden to Brooklyn by its owner.

Police on both sides of the river tried to halt the stream of adventurers, but with little success. Other ladder entrepreneurs had appeared, and now there were more spots where a person could get onto the ice than policemen to block them.

Not everyone had an easy crossing. Many slipped on the treacherous ice or were blown over by the still-fierce wind. A few of the elderly adventurers had to be carried to shore. For over an hour and a half, people and animals paraded from one shore to the other. While no one kept an official count, the policemen on duty that day estimated that between 1,500 and 3,000 walked across the river.

The cheerful mood of the crowd began to subside just after 9 A.M. That was when a deep, ominous grumbling began coming from the ice. The tide was beginning to shift, pushing at the ice to shove it downriver. Meanwhile, three powerful tugs had been ordered out to batter

These tugboats are ramming their way through the ice to get river traffic moving once again. One man is being hauled on board the nearest tug, while a nattily dressed businessman stranded on a nearby chunk of ice waits anxiously to be rescued. (AUTHOR'S COLLECTION)

and break the floe in order to free up the river for navigation. When those operating the ladder-climbing concessions noticed this, they raised their prices to twenty-five cents.

Those on the ice realized the danger they were in and hurried to the closest shore. All of the dogs must have sensed something also, because they fled the ice as well. A large squad of police arrived and began ordering the ladders pulled up and watchers away from the ice. "Very many refused to obey," a reporter for the *Sun* noted. "When the ladders were taken away, they let themselves down from the piers. . . . They thirsted for glory."

Just then, the tide turned and began exerting immense pressure downriver. The giant cake of ice began to move very slowly. "There were over a hundred persons on the ice at this moment," the *Sun* reporter went on. "Most of them broke into a run. Loud were the cries [by those on the riverbank] to get to the shore."

When the ice broke free and began moving seaward, there were between forty and fifty people still on it. The ice came close to the Fulton Ferry pier and some of the stranded tried to grab hold, but the pilings were too slippery. They were close enough that the *Sun* reporter could see that "some exchanged cool jokes with those on the docks. One quietly asked to have a tug sent down for him; another requested a stove; still another shouted that he'd cable from Europe. . . . One man sank down on his knees and prayed."

The ice inched along and collided with a collection of piers on the New York City side. There was a horrible crunching sound as ice met wood, and then the floe came to a shivering stop. In the few minutes it was lodged there, men on the docks lowered down ladders and ropes and managed to pull almost everyone up to safety. Then the floe broke free and continued downriver.

There were still a number of men trapped on smaller chunks of ice heading toward New York Bay and the open sea. Three bobbed about near the Brooklyn shore, while five were close to Manhattan.

The *Sun* reporter took up the story of the three Brooklyn men. "The ice cracked merrily. Then it bulged up, separated and each young man was launched upon a separate cake of ice. The men shouted frantically and waved their arms. . . . Two of the men were on neighboring ice cakes. One finally made a dangerous jump to the cake nearer the shore on which the other stood. The crowd shouted approval, [and] told them to keep their hearts."

A rope with a rock attached to it was eventually tossed to these men and they were hauled to shore and rescued.

"The other young man, who was irreproachably dressed and carried a satchel, was on a cake scarcely twenty-five feet in diameter. He ran from edge to edge, till each time he nearly slipped in the water, and showed such terror that terror was communicated to those on shore."

Farther and farther out the desperate man drifted, and many watchers felt he would be lost. Then the tugboat *S. E. Babcock* managed to plow through a large chunk of ice and swing in close enough for the man to be brought on board.

Meanwhile, the five men near Manhattan were floating out rapidly. Three were on a rather large slab of ice, while two were each on cakes that the *Sun* reporter said were "the size of door mats."

First, a tug nudged the large floe into shore until it hit a wharf and the three men leaped off. Then the tug went after the two last floaters. When they were finally hauled up and safe "the thousands of men on the riverside and the Bridge yelled their applause in rounds of cheers and screams."

In addition to the cheers, Tuesday morning was a time of tears and much worry in all areas hit by the blizzard. It was when family and friends began searching for those who were missing or who hadn't been heard from since Monday. When concerned relatives of Long Island potato farmer Sam Randall found his house empty that morning, they immediately set out for the barn, assuming he had decided to stay there for the night. While plowing through the deep snow, they stumbled across his frozen body.

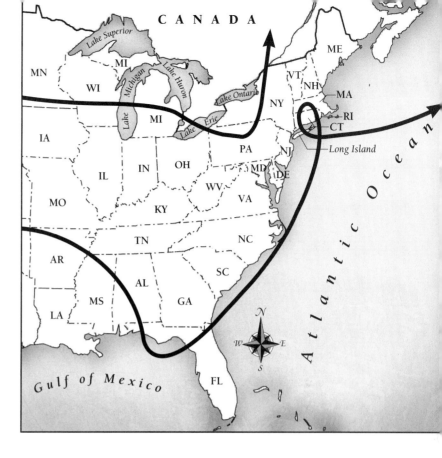

This map shows the complete route of the two storms that produced the Great Blizzard of 1888. The southern storm eventually headed across the Atlantic and dumped great quantities of snow on northern England and other parts of Europe, where it became known as the American Storm.

Outside of Albany, railroad officials were compiling a list of the passengers aboard the burned-out train from Buffalo when someone remembered the attractive young woman. Since no one knew where she was, crews were immediately dispatched to search along the tracks. Several hours later, Sara Wilson's body was uncovered, still clutching her Empress Eugénie hat with its pretty red feather.

James Marshall's parents weren't particularly worried when he failed to return home on Monday night. They assumed he had stayed at the Singer factory in Elizabeth. They were concerned on Tuesday morning, but without telephone or telegraph service in their area, there wasn't

In areas where snow was a frequent visitor, towns often didn't bother to dig their streets clean. This snow roller was used in Brattleboro, Vermont, to flatten snow so sleighs could travel easily. (BRATTLEBORO P.H.O.T.O.)

much they could do but wait. They would have been shocked to know that James had kept up his dogged race against death all night and was even then still plodding along, desperately hoping to be discovered.

In Connecticut, the older brother of Legrand and Gurdon Chapell woke up that Tuesday and set out by sleigh to join the rest of the family at Grandma's. When he arrived, he was asked where his little brothers were, and it became instantly clear that they were lost somewhere in the snow.

An hour later, every nearby neighbor had been asked to join in a search for the boys. Falling snow and wind had obliterated their tracks, but it was assumed they had attempted to cross the fields between their house and their grandmother's. At around noon, Legrand's mittens and cap were found near a very large snowdrift and the worst was assumed.

The searchers were discouraged, but decided that they had to at least find the boys' bodies. But how were they going to do that in such a vast area of snow?

An elderly man who had been in several winter searches suggested that they use bean poles to poke through the crusted snow. He had brought one with him and began demonstrating how to jab it into the snow and poke around with it. When they hit a body, he told those assembled, it would feel softer than the hard ground nearby. He jabbed a few more times, when, from deep within the snow, they heard a very faint cry of "Ouch!"

Frantic digging followed and within minutes both boys were uncovered from the snow cave Gurdon had hollowed out for them twenty-two hours before. The boys were whisked to a warm kitchen where their stiff clothes were cut from their bodies. Next, they were plopped into a tub of tepid water, and then each was given a large dose of whiskey. Even though the boys were beginning to come around, a concerned neighbor insisted that they be wrapped in a sheet smeared with molasses to completely ward off frostbite.

The boys survived and lived long lives, during which they often told of how they had survived the Great Blizzard of 1888. Legrand vividly recalled how he and Gurdon had clung to each other in their cave and how Gurdon had said, "We'll never get out of here. We will die, but I can't carry you out and I can't go and leave you alone."

By the time Legrand and Gurdon were found, the snow had finally stopped falling everywhere. The northern storm was now over Greenland and no longer exerting much influence on weather in the United States. The southern storm, the one that had circled around, was over the outer tip of Long Island by 3 P.M. The storm would continue turning, then head across the Atlantic toward Europe, picking up moisture as it made its journey. When it hit Europe with its high winds and snow, it was dubbed the "American Storm."

As the storm lessened, then stopped in the United States, efforts to clear roads, sidewalks, and railroad tracks intensified, as did the search for the missing. But most people in cities were far from out of danger. Mothers with buckets trudged from store to store in search of milk for their children, but found none available. In New York, the tiny supply of milk available was reserved for the better restaurants, where the price of a glass quickly went up to seventy-five cents.

Other food prices also zoomed up. On the previous Friday, the cost of a chicken had been seven cents; on Tuesday they went for twenty-five cents. Eggs jumped from twenty-five cents to forty cents a dozen, while butter more than doubled in price to thirty cents a pound. A steak

One way to cope with unshoveled streets was to poke fun at the politicians responsible for snow removal. This particular cartoon appeared in a New York City paper, but people in other cities held the same view of their politicians. (AUTHOR'S COLLECTION)

At a recent meeting of the Board of Aldermen, it was Resolved to let the streets take care of themselves, as heretofore.

that cost sixteen cents a pound was now blizzard-priced at twenty-two cents; spring lamb went from twenty-eight cents to thirty cents a pound. These prices may seem extremely low to us, but back in 1888, someone with an unskilled job might be making between three and twenty dollars per week. Even an increase of a few pennies per pound could mean the difference between eating and not eating to a poor family.

The same leap in price happened with coal. Before the blizzard, it cost one cent a pound. By Tuesday, the price stood at two and a half cents and was rising. The poor might be able to purchase five or ten pounds of coal, but such a meager supply wouldn't last very long in a stove going throughout the day and night.

There was little the poorest in the city could do but suffer. Church and private shelters were already full and struggling to care for those presently in their charge. Police stations were likewise jammed and had no real food supplies to hand out. The city itself provided very little in the way of direct help to those in need.

In fact, the only known attempt at widespread relief came from a wealthy realtor, P. M. Wilson. Wilson owned a number of buildings on Broadway as well as large tracts of land on the West Side of the city. He knew from his visits to the West Side that the poor there must be suffering terribly, and before noon, placards began appearing which read:

ATTENTION!

FREE COAL TO POOR FAMILIES IN THE NEIGHBORHOOD WILL BE SUPPLIED AFTER 12:00 NOON, MARCH 13, 1888, AT THE ENGINE ROOM OF THE ROSS BUILDING, HUDSON STREET, CORNER BANK STREET.

BY ORDER OF,

P. M. WILSON

During the coal shortage, a man in Brooklyn uses a boat to haul coal. (MUSEUM OF THE CITY OF NEW YORK)

A long line of needy people soon formed outside the door to the engine room — mothers cradling infants, little children, men out of work, and even elderly men and women came. Each brought a pail, bucket, or sack to haul away a few pounds of the precious fuel.

Wilson's kindness helped several hundred families have coal enough for a warm home and a hot meal. But by Tuesday night, countless individuals and families throughout the area hit by the blizzard had much to endure. Food was so scarce in New Haven, Connecticut, that a man wrote in his diary: "We are desperate. No milk. Only condensed milk and that is going fast. All fresh meat gone. Groceries shut. Restaurants dark. Nothing to eat. Nothing. What will my poor children do?"

EIGHT

IT IS ONLY A SNOWSTORM

The Great Blizzard officially ended on Wednesday, March 14. An additional two inches of snow fell on upstate New York and New England, but it was a gentle fall with little accompanying wind. Skies throughout the storm region cleared, and temperatures from Delaware all the way up to Canada rose. Both Philadelphia and Boston recorded a balmy 40 degrees. As quickly as it had disappeared, the warm weather returned.

Down in Lewes, Delaware, the nice weather brought out crowds who gawked at the devastation in the harbor. The long steel pier had a 200-foot-long chunk ripped out of it, and boats and ships were strewn about everywhere, some on land, some wallowing in shallow water. Despite the dangers, the captains and crews of these vessels hurried to get aboard them. Salvage laws stated that both the craft and its contents belonged to the first person to take possession of it.

Just outside of Lewes, a very hungry John Marshall breathed a sigh of relief — and said a prayer of thanks — when a rescue crew finally located and dug out his train. While the vast majority of trains would be moving on Wednesday, a small number — estimated at between

Breakthrough! A line of engines coupled together finally forces its way through a snowdrift so it can get to a stranded train. (AUTHOR'S COLLECTION)

twenty and thirty trains — would remain snowbound until Friday. Most of these missing trains were either in very remote areas, or they belonged to railroad companies that did not want to spend money to rescue them.

On Wednesday in New York City, a plow pulled by a team of twenty-eight horses and assisted by over 100 Italian shovelers finally opened up the 59th Street and Spuyten Duyvil cuts. Within minutes, one train after another began limping in, and Grand Central Depot gradually came back to life. Chauncey Depew expressed satisfaction that his railroad was running once again, and then, after issuing a few orders, he left the office. He would have to face many disgruntled patrons in the days ahead, but for the moment, all he wanted was to be at home and asleep in his own bed.

In addition to passenger trains, others carrying the mail and desperately needed supplies of beef, chicken, and dairy products began pulling into stations everywhere on Wednesday. The widespread famine some had feared never materialized, though many grocers kept prices very high until the end of the following week.

While the predicted famine was averted, another sort of disaster began to unfold in isolated rural areas. Train service to Poughkeepsie, New York, did not return to normal for three weeks. During that time, local dairy farmers were forced to destroy tens of thousands of gallons of milk and thousands of pounds of butter. Over in Pennsylvania, the lack of transportation led to the layoff of over 10,000 coal and iron miners. In addition, many rural factories were also forced to shut down temporarily as well. Either they couldn't get the necessary materials to make their products or the fuel to run their machines, or else they had no way to get what they made to market. It would take weeks, and in some cases months, for the dairy farmers, miners, and workers to recover from the financial setbacks caused by the blizzard.

The hardships suffered by these people, as well as by the poor, were largely ignored by most citizens, politicians, and the newspapers. It seemed that everyone wanted to put the storm behind them and get back to normal as quickly as possible. The New York *Sun* crowed: WE ARE ON TOP NOW. THE TOWN HAS GOT THE BLIZZARD DOWN. NO LONGER ISOLATED. Another New York City paper proudly announced: DIGGING OUT OF IT. THE BIG CITY GETS UP AND SHAKES ITSELF. YOU CAN GET AROUND NOW.

Such boasts were made everywhere hit by the blizzard. A Connecticut paper said firmly: FLAKES HAVE LOST THEIR GRIP, while in Vermont the claim was, THE BLOCKADE BROKEN. RAILROAD TRAFFIC AT LEAST PARTIALLY RESUMED IN VERMONT. Gone was the sense that the storm was invincible and that humans were helpless. The Waterbury, Connecticut, paper

Shortly after the snow stopped falling, these two men attempted to clear a path across a street. The wind took most of their work and tossed it back into their faces. (AUTHOR'S COLLECTION)

made it clear who was now boss: PUSHED THROUGH! WATERBURY HEAD AND SHOULDERS ABOVE THE DRIFTS. MEN WHO CANNOT BE DOWNED IN THIS WAY. THE SNOW BEATING A VERY HASTY RETREAT.

While the newspapers trumpeted the storm's demise, people used humor to show they had not been defeated by the blizzard. A prankster placed a placard on a particularly huge drift near New York City's Madison Square that read: THIS SNOW IS ABSOLUTELY FREE! PLEASE TAKE A SAMPLE!

Several blocks away, a shopkeeper, frustrated that he could not find anyone to shovel his snow, left this sign outside his place of business: IMPORTANT! EXPENSIVE DIAMOND RING LOST UNDER THIS SNOW DRIFT! FINDERS KEEPERS! START DIGGING! YOU MAY BE THE LUCKY WINNER!

Up in Albany, a florist took his unsold flowers and stuck them in a snowdrift to resemble a hill of beautiful springtime flowers. A sign on the drift warned pedestrians: DON'T PICK THE FLOWERS.

It seemed as if every city and most towns had some youthful pranksters as well. In Albany, a group of boys with excess energy dug a 100-foot-long path up the sidewalk and around the corner. Unsuspecting adults wouldn't realize that the path came to a dead end until they came face-to-face with an 80-foot-tall drift. A slight variation on the "path to nowhere" was found in New York City. On turning the corner, adults discovered the path narrowing until it was just wide enough for a child's thin body to squeeze through.

The brave words and humor helped people unwind from the tension and terror of the storm's assault. It also distracted them from the massive chore of digging out. It was all posturing, of course, and all one had to do to know this was to look around.

William Inglis was in a cheerful mood as his pilot schooner *Colt*

This resident of Danbury, Connecticut, pauses for a moment before digging his way through a daunting pile of snow outside his home. (CONNECTICUT HISTORICAL SOCIETY)

neared shore. "We all thanked God that we were alive," he would write. Besides, he had a great adventure story to tell his readers.

As the schooner neared land, Inglis realized for the first time the true extent of the storm's devastation. Numerous damaged ships were being towed in by tugs, while broken and battered boats could be seen in all directions. "We saw three wrecked pilot-boats ashore [near] Sandy Hook, another in Gravesend, and poor No. 2, with nothing but her masts showing below the Bay Ridge pier. . . ."

Just then, the steward called them below for lunch, the first hot meal they had had since Sunday. "As we fell to sharply, a tug passed by one quarter to windward. The man at the wheel hailed her for news."

The answer was shouted in a loud voice that everyone below heard clearly. "Nine pilot boats wrecked." They had all been fierce competitors of the *Colt* for business, but they were also friends and neighbors. "Big Fairgreaves pushed his plate away and went on deck. There were tears coming out of the corners of his eyes. None of the rest of us ate any more."

In truth, the cruelty of the storm had not really ended. On that Wednesday morning, a Staten Island farmer was out looking for stray cattle when he discovered a young man stumbling around and around one of his haystacks. It was James Marshall. Amazingly, he had managed to keep moving, sometimes running, sometimes walking, sometimes crawling on his hands and knees, since Monday evening. He was mumbling incoherently by the time the farmer got him to a doctor.

Despite Marshall's attempt to shelter them, both his friends had died from exposure. As for Marshall, an article in the New York *World* told about his own terrible fate: "Dr. E. D. Conley, who is attending Marshall, says he will be taken to the infirmary this morning where his hands and feet will be amputated."

Nor was the blizzard's danger really over, even with the sky brighten-

Hundreds of small boats were caught in the storm and capsized by the gigantic waves. This drawing shows one of the few people who managed to drag himself ashore. (MUSEUM OF THE CITY OF NEW YORK)

ing and temperatures going up. Responding to a rumor that a tidal wave had destroyed a hotel at Coney Island, the New York *Eagle* sent out twenty-one-year-old cub reporter Richard C. Reilly that Wednesday.

Reilly managed to get aboard a train clearing the tracks to Brighton Beach, and from there he struggled through one mile of deep snow to Coney Island. The storm had severely damaged the town, but there was no evidence that a tidal wave had struck. After thoroughly exploring the area and talking with numerous residents, Reilly decided to head back with his story.

Even though the train had already left and darkness was approaching, Reilly refused to give up. He wanted his story to appear before any other paper could beat him out. He found a stable and rented a horse and sleigh (for a whopping thirty-five dollars!), then set off.

All day, Reilly had taken detailed notes, and he did so on his way back to the office, too. His last entry was made near Patrick Maher's

Many bodies were pulled from the snow and transported to the morgue. Relatives had to identify the body before it could be released for burial. (AUTHOR'S COLLECTION)

farm. Reilly's unconscious body was found the next day lying in a snowbank. No one really knows what happened to him, but detectives hired by the *Eagle* suggested that the day's strenuous physical effort had brought on a heart attack. Despite efforts to revive him — which included placing hot bricks at his feet and thirteen hot-water bottles around his body — Reilly died without regaining consciousness. The blizzard had claimed another victim.

There were many other victims. Most historians place the number of those killed at around 400, but this number must certainly be too low. On average, 400 people were buried every week in New York City. When burials began again on the Friday after the storm, over 800 bodies were brought to the area's cemeteries. This additional number does not include the hundreds killed at sea on foreign ships (who were never counted on official lists in the United States) or those who perished in cities and towns in other states. Nor does this number include the many individuals who died from heart attacks or other illnesses brought on by exposure to cold or from shoveling wet, heavy snow.

One such victim was the unstoppable Roscoe Conkling. The day after collapsing at the door of the New York Club, Conkling went downtown to be interviewed by the press. He talked at length about his adventure, but then went home with a terrible headache. His condition worsened, but the ever stubborn Conkling refused to follow his doctor's orders to rest. He died on April 18. His death certificate stated that he died from mastoiditis and pneumonia, but everyone who read Conkling's obituary knew it was the Great Blizzard that had done him in.

There have been numerous winter storms to rival and even surpass the Blizzard of 1888 in snowfall and wind velocity. The American Midwest had seen many savage blizzards that whipped down from northwest Canada with blinding speed and awful intensity. One struck on December 21, 1836, that plunged temperatures by 50 degrees in a matter of minutes. An Illinois settler named John Moses wrote about the instant cold that hit his area: "The water in the little ponds in the road froze in waves, sharp-edged and pointed, as the gale had blown it. . . . Men caught out on horseback were frozen to their saddles, and had to be lifted off and carried to the fire to be thawed apart. Two young men were frozen to death near Rushville. One of them was found with his back against a tree, with his horse's bridle over his arm, and his horse frozen in front of him."

During the winter of 1880–1881, the Plains were hit by a series of particularly fierce blizzards — one a week, each lasting three or more days, from January through April. These storms stopped railroad service for seventy-nine straight days and dumped 11 feet of snow in the Dakota Territory. In January of 1888, a blizzard earned the nickname the "schoolchildren's storm" because it struck the Nebraska and

Dakota Territory with such speed that children were caught on their way home from school.

Even in our own times, we have seen killer blizzards more powerful than the Blizzard of 1888. The Superstorm of 1993 roared across the eastern United States from March 12 to 14, dumping record-breaking amounts of snow in all areas. The *National Disaster Survey Report* called the 1993 storm "among the greatest nontropical weather events to affect the Nation in modern times." The report went on to note that the storm inconvenienced over 100 million people and that, even with ample warning of its approach, over 200 people died in it.

Despite these and other historic storms, the Blizzard of 1888 is still the one most written about in our nation's history. Why is this?

First, the sudden onslaught of the storm and the way it completely shut down every big and small city from Virginia on up into Canada traumatized millions of people. The fear they felt during the storm, and the relief at having survived it, lingered in their memories for many years afterward.

In itself, this is not unusual, since every natural disaster leaves survivors with similar feelings and vivid impressions. The Blizzard of 1888 differed because it was recorded in great detail by the many newspapers then in existence. Adding to this abundance of information were the more than 1,200 personal accounts collected over the years by an organization known as the Society of Blizzard Men and Blizzard Ladies of 1888, and now housed at the New-York Historical Society.

A massive written record plays an important role in sustaining the memory and myths of any storm. But the Blizzard of 1888 is recalled today primarily because of the long-term impact it had on the way we live in the United States.

New York City had been completely paralyzed — and embarrassed —

by the storm. As a consequence, *The New York Times* pointed out, "people vexed at the collapse of all the principal means of intercommunication and transportation became reflective, and the result was a general expression of opinion that an immediate and radical improvement was imperative."

This was easier said than done because changes in the way New York or other cities operated required legislation. And getting any law passed was a complicated and tricky process. Because of this, Mayor Hewitt began by going after a fairly easy target.

Moments after the snow stopped falling on Wednesday, he ordered companies to put their wires underground and to take down their poles. He was able to act so quickly in this instance because the necessary legislation was already in place. Even so, most companies simply ignored Hewitt and began putting up their overladen poles again. One company even sued the city, claiming the law was a violation of its constitutional guarantee of freedom of speech.

But the blizzard had fostered in the public a mood for change. People remembered a prestorm city encircled and bound up by thousands of wires, and they remembered writhing live wires dancing on their streets and sidewalks during the storm. It didn't take a genius to see that underground wires made sense. Public opinion was further aroused when a Western Union lineman was electrocuted and, as one historian tells it, "thousands watched as the body dangled from overhead lines for nearly an hour, its mouth spitting blue flame." By 1894, all wires in New York City had been banished underground, and other cities — including Washington, D.C.; Boston; Albany; and Buffalo, to name a few — followed its example.

Snapped poles and high-voltage wires weren't the only thing to anger citizens in New York and other cities or to cause a change in the way things were done. Flying debris — from store signs, household garbage, and broken glass to newspapers, coal, and horse manure — had all endangered pedestrians during the storm.

It would take months and years of public debate and squabbling, but eventually a series of tough new ordinances emerged. Containers holding coal, garbage, and other items were banned from sidewalks, while store and home owners were required to clean up the streets and sidewalks in front of their property. The size and types of signs were regulated as well, and some of the first antilittering laws were drawn up. In short, many activities once considered the private affairs of a citizen became matters for public concern and legislation.

The blizzard also caused Alfred Ely Beach's 1849 dream of an underground railway system to be set in motion at long last. The powerful aboveground transportation companies and their political cronies would continue to call a subway system a costly and unnecessary expense. But the hundreds of thousands of voting commuters who had been trapped during the storm felt otherwise.

The first subway line in New York City, opened in 1904 by August Belmont's Interborough Rapid Transit Company (the IRT), initially covered 22 miles and was an immediate success. Soon, it was carrying over 600,000 people a year, in rain, summer heat, and, as Alfred Ely Beach had said all along, even during snowstorms. Other cities, including Newark, New Jersey, Chicago, Boston, and Philadelphia, would also install underground rail systems in the years following the blizzard.

Another profound change was in the way people and their governments viewed snow. In New York City alone, the cost to businesses for the three-day blizzard was estimated at between $2,500,000 and $3,000,000. Even with 17,000 shovelers, snow removal was slow and businesses couldn't bring in needed supplies or send out what they produced. Complaints about the slow clearing of streets persisted long after the snow

The storm is over and hundreds of impatient passengers are lined up and waiting, but these horse carriages still aren't moving at this station on Bowery Street. (AUTHOR'S COLLECTION)

had melted, and were one important reason why Mayor Hewitt was voted out of office the following November.

It didn't take city politicians long to realize that their jobs depended on a quick and efficient response to future snowstorms and other disasters. Plans were drawn up to meet future emergencies, no matter how unusual they might be. These plans included details on what might happen, how the city should respond, the costs involved, and the necessary workforce.

Giant icicles dangle from the surrounding roofs as this Italian work gang in Newark shovels snow to the side of the street and begins spreading dirt so horses have better footing. (NEW JERSEY HISTORICAL SOCIETY)

The notion that the work of the city could be done by temporary help was also rejected, and more permanent workers were hired by the city to clean streets, pick up garbage, and remove snow. One interesting result of this change was that thousands of recently arrived Italian immigrants found secure jobs with the city.

New York City wasn't the only place to change as a result of the blizzard. Following the storm, no city would be built or managed that did not have detailed emergency plans and the workers available to carry them out. These changes did not happen overnight. The increased obligations all cost money, and many people objected to the resulting rise in taxes. Numerous efforts were made to stall the necessary legislation, especially when it came to helping the poor. Change did come, however. In fact, only one major city — Detroit — still does not plow snow from its residential streets. But the notion that a city has no responsibility for its people and businesses in an emergency died with the blizzard.

The upset that followed the storm seemed unusually strong in Washington, D.C. The nation's capital had been completely cut off from the rest of the country from Sunday through Wednesday. During that time, President Grover Cleveland and his wife had been stranded at their country home outside of Washington, without any way to contact his cabinet or the Congress.

One senator's highly emotional speech about the danger posed by the Blizzard of 1888 ended with this declaration: "We cannot control the elements. We cannot prevent another blizzard. We can protect our communications. All wires now running overhead must be placed underground in the urban areas and thus shielded from the caprices of nature. Not only are the overhead wires unsafe and unsightly — they are a damned menace to the security of the United States of America."

What if the country had been invaded while the storm was raging?

Brattleboro postman Spencer W. Knight tried to deliver mail during the blizzard but was forced to give up early on. Here he is after the sidewalk had been shoveled through wave after wave of snow. (BRATTLEBORO P.H.O.T.O.)

senators wanted to know. What if assassins had killed the president while communications were down?

Like all other cities, Washington, D.C., responded by passing laws and regulations designed to keep streets open and telephone and telegraph wires safe. Congress, however, wasn't finished. It heaped particular scorn on the Signal Corps's failure to predict the storm and demanded to know why.

When the head of the Washington Weather Station, General Adolphus Greely, tried to shrug off the storm as "a somewhat unusual class of storm," he was severely criticized.

The first chief forecaster for the fledgling National Weather Service,

Snowdrifts dwarf a line of pedestrians in Hartford, Connecticut. (CONNECTICUT HISTORICAL SOCIETY)

Professor Cleveland Abbe, was more direct in assessing why his people had failed to predict the storm's intensity. "The element that fooled us was the ocean winds, about which we never have any warning," he said. "You see, we know so little anyway, and there is so much more of which we are and must be ignorant. . . . We are utterly ignorant of what is going on to the east of us, and overhead."

Abbe's confession of ignorance had several effects. Control of the Signal Corps was taken away from the army and handed over to the Department of Agriculture in 1891. Its name was changed to the less military one of the United States Weather Bureau.

The second change had to do with the Weather Bureau's mission. The Signal Corps focused on issuing daily weather indications and advance warnings about storms. The Weather Bureau expanded its role of responsibility to learning meteorological laws, hoping that knowledge about how and why weather happens would improve its ability to more accurately predict it. With these changes went an ever-increasing budget.

This change in the way the nation approached the weather was a significant start, and would eventually lead to the use of radar, high-speed electronic computers, and satellites in forecasting weather patterns. The theories about the clash of warm and cold air masses high up in the atmosphere and their effect on the weather (put forward by Norwegian Vilhelm Bjerknes and his son Jacob) also lay in the future. Today, weather forecasting for the following day has an accuracy rate of 95 percent.

Finally, the practice of closing the Bureau for the Sabbath was abolished. In the future, the Weather Bureau would stay open and alert twenty-four hours a day, seven days a week. No longer would the country be open to a surprise change in the weather.

What mattered most at the close of the nineteenth century was that the flaws revealed by the Blizzard of 1888 had been addressed and solved. There would be no chance for future killer storms to catch the nation unprepared. Or so people back then believed.

On September 8, 1900, a hurricane tore apart Galveston, Texas, and killed an estimated 6,000 people. The Weather Bureau correctly predicted the storm, but failed to take into account the effect of the high tide. Thirty-eight years later, the Bureau forecasted a severe windstorm for Long Island and southern New England, but incorrectly judged the storm's speed. Over 600 people perished as a result.

And even as the new millennium dawned, nature flexed its muscles once again. On January 24, 2000, a storm hit the East Coast with record-breaking snowfalls from North Carolina up into Massachusetts. Many cities were unable to cope with the snow and came to a frozen halt. North Carolina was so completely paralyzed it had to call out the National Guard to help clear its roads, while in Washington, D.C., the federal government was forced to close most of its offices for two days.

The storm had developed in the south and wandered out into the Atlantic where forecasters expected it to die. But, like the Blizzard of 1888, this recent storm shocked everyone when it turned and came back onshore. In a front-page article, *The New York Times* noted that "officials at the National Weather Service acknowledged . . . that their forecasts had failed to predict the size, intensity, or course of the storm."

The lesson is clear: No matter how many pieces of equipment we develop, no matter how many ways we try to predict weather patterns, nature always has the potential to surprise and overwhelm us.

Probably the best summation about the Blizzard of 1888 — and all other killer storms — was made in a Hartford *Courant* editorial while the snow was still fresh on the ground.

"It is the boasting and progressive Nineteenth Century that is paralyzed," the editorial said, "while the slow-going Eighteenth would have taken such an experience without a ruffle. It is our own 'advantages' that have gone back on us.

"But lo . . . there comes a storm [and] there is no railroad, no telegraph, no horse car, no milk, no delivery of food at the door. We starve in the midst of plenty. . . . It warns us to be discreet and temperate in our boasting. It is only a snowstorm, but it has downed us."

NOTES ON SOURCES
AND RELATED READING MATERIAL

When I was five years old, a great, howling snowstorm struck the northeast coast of the United States. The snow piled up so high that our town had to use long-necked steam shovels to clear the streets. But what I remembered most vividly was a walk I took with my mother and older brother shortly after the storm ended.

We were going to a friend's house, which was only two blocks away and a journey we had made many times before. At one point, my mother and brother were 20 feet ahead of me, breaking a trail through waist-high snow. I decided this was the perfect time for a little adventure. So off I scurried — up a neighbor's driveway and across his backyard. My plan was to travel parallel to the sidewalk through all the backyards and beat my mother and brother to the end of the block.

Everything went well for several backyards. Then I climbed up a wire fence and leaped into the next yard — only this time the earth dropped out from under me. I had landed in a deep drift of powdery white snow and found myself in over my head!

I clawed and kicked at the snow to get free, without success. I tried to pull myself up and out of my snowy trap, but each time the walls caved in around me. I cleared the snow away from my head, but I couldn't escape its grasp or even move my feet an inch. And the more I flailed and screamed for help, the more tired my legs and arms became. Worse, when I quieted down for a second to rest, the only sound I heard was the lonely moan of the wind. No one, I thought, was ever going to rescue me.

I was probably stuck in that drift for only a minute longer, but it felt like an eternity. And you can imagine how happy I was to finally hear

my mother and brother answer one of my feeble calls. My little encounter with snow came flooding back to me in great detail one day as I pored over more than 1,200 letters of reminiscence written by members of the Society of Blizzard Men and Blizzard Ladies.

These can be found in the manuscript collection of the New-York Historical Society and are the source of most of the personal recollections I've quoted. A limited number of these recollections appeared in Hugh Flick's "The Great Blizzard and the Blizzard Men of 1888,"

The Blizzard Men and Blizzard Ladies of 1888 gather at the Hotel Pennsylvania in New York City on March 12, 1938, to celebrate the fiftieth anniversary of the Great Blizzard. (NEW-YORK HISTORICAL SOCIETY)

published in the *New-York Historical Society Quarterly Bulletin,* vol. 19 (1935), 31. Whenever possible, I have credited the author of the quotes by name, but many of these letters are unsigned.

Several individual's stories, as well as their quotes, come from sources other than the New-York Historical Society's archives. Information about Sara Wilson and A. C. Chadbourne comes from *The Great Blizzard of 1888,* by Samuel Meredith Strong (New York: Privately printed, 1938); Chauncey Depew details his own struggle with the blizzard in his autobiography, *My Memories of Eighty Years* (New York: Charles Scribner's Sons, 1922); information about Roscoe Conkling was found in William H. Hoy's article, "Roscoe Conkling Nearly Dead," which appeared in the New York *Sun* on March 14, 1888, as well as Samuel Meredith Strong's history of the blizzard (see above).

A number of histories of the Great Blizzard of 1888 proved to be especially helpful in reconstructing scenes and events. *The Blizzard of '88* by Mary Cable (New York: Atheneum, 1988) has a strong focus on the dangers faced by commuting workers due to the shutdown of public transportation. Irving Werstein's *The Blizzard of '88* (New York: Thomas Y. Crowell, 1960) makes the plight of the urban poor especially clear and dramatic. *Blizzard! The Great Storm of '88* by Judd Caplovich (Vernon, Vermont: VeRo Publishing Company, 1987) does an extremely good job of covering the storm in areas outside of New York City, plus it contains hundreds of photographs and newspaper clippings.

Other sources consulted were: *New York in the Blizzard,* by Napoleon Augustus Jennings (New York: Rogers and Sherwood, 1888); "The Mighty Blizzard of March 1888," by Edward Oxford, *American History Illustrated* 23 (March 1988), 11–19; and "The Great Blizzard of '88," by Nat Brandt, *American Heritage* 108 (1977), 32.

Technical information about the storm and the U.S. Signal Corps comes from a number of valuable sources: *The Great Storm Off the Atlantic Coast of the United States, March 11th–14th 1888,* by Everett Hayden (Washington, D.C.: Government Printing Office, 1888); *Braving the Elements: The Stormy History of American Weather,* by David Laskin (New York: Anchor Books, Doubleday, 1996); *Snow in America,* by Bernard Mergen (Washington and London: Smithsonian Institution Press, 1997); *A Century of Weather Service,* by Patrick Hughes (New York: Gordon and Branch, 1970); *A History of the United States Weather Bureau,* by Donald R. Whitnah (Urbana, Illinois: University of Illinois Press, 1961); "The Great Storm of March 11–14, 1888," by General Adolphus W. Greely, *National Geographic* 1 (May 1888); "The Blizzard of '88," by Patrick Hughes, *Weatherwise* (1981), 250; and "Summary of the Blizzard of '88 Centennial Meeting," by Mark L. Kramer and Gary Solomon, *Bulletin of the American Meteorological Society* 69 (August 1988), 981–83.

Other weather-related material comes from the following sources: *American Weather,* by General Adolphus W. Greely (New York: Dodd, Mead and Company, 1888); *Great Storms,* by L. G. C. Laughton (New York: William F. Payson, 1931); *Early American Winters,* by David Ludlum (Boston: American Meteorological Society, 1966); and *Great Gales and Dire Disasters,* by Edward Rowe Snow (New York: Dodd, Mead and Company, 1952).

Because the Blizzard of 1888 had such a powerful effect on New York City and its citizens, much of this book takes place there. Information and details about the city's history, infrastructure, and day-to-day operation come from the following titles: *Labyrinths of Iron: Subways in History, Myth, Art, Technology, and War,* by Bobrick Benson (New York: Henry Holt and Company, 1986); *Gotham: A History of New York City to 1898,* by Edwin G. Burrows and Mike Wallace (New York: Oxford University Press, 1999); *Under the Sidewalks of New York,* by Brian J. Cudahy (Brattleboro, Vermont: Stephen Greene Press, 1979); *The Historical Atlas of New York City,* by Eric Homberger (New York: Henry

Shovelers in front of the Hotel Pennsylvania pause a moment to have their picture snapped.

Holt and Company, 1994); *722 Miles: The Building of the Subways and How They Transformed New York,* by Clifton Hood (New York: Simon & Schuster, 1993); *The Way It Was: New York, 1850–1890,* by Clarence P. Hornung (New York: Schocken Books, 1977); *The Encyclopedia of*

New York City, by Kenneth T. Jackson (New York and New Haven: Yale University Press and The New-York Historical Society, 1995); *Under the City Streets,* by Pamela Jones (New York: Holt, Rinehart and Winston, 1978); *The Columbia Historical Portrait of New York,* by John A. Kouwenhoven (New York: Harper and Row, 1953); *The Building of Manhattan: How Manhattan Was Built Over Ground and Underground from the Dutch Settlers to the Skyscraper,* by Donald A. Mackey (New York: Harper and Row, 1987); and *Fares, Please! A Popular History of Trolleys, Horse-Cars, Street-Cars, Buses, Elevateds, and Subways,* by John Anderson Miller (New York: D. Appleton-Century, 1941).

Information about the poor and homeless was obtained from the following sources: *Darkness and Daylight: or Lights and Shadows of New York Life,* by Helen Campbell, Thomas W. Knox, and Thomas Byrnes (Hartford, Connecticut: A. D. Worthington, 1892); *The Tenement House Problem,* by Robert W. DeForest and Lawrence Veiller (New York: Macmillan Co., 1903); *La Storia: Five Centuries of the Italian American Experience,* by Jerre Mangione and Ben Morreale (New York: Harper-Perennial, HarperCollins Publishers, 1992); *How the Other Half Lives,* by Jacob Riis (New York: Charles Scribner's Sons, 1890); and *New York: Sunshine and Shade,* by Roger Whitehouse (New York: Harper and Row, 1974).

Finally, concern about potential food and coal shortages were voiced in a number of newspapers: *The Philadelphia Inquirer*, March 13 and 14, 1888; *The New York Times*, March 14, 1888; the New York *Sun*, March 15, 1888; the Boston *Daily Globe*, March 15, 1888; and the *Torrington (VT) Register*, March 17, 1888.

INDEX

PAGE NUMBERS IN BOLD INDICATE ILLUSTRATIONS

Abbe, Cleveland, 122

Algeo, James, 14–15, 36

American Bank Note Company, 36

Anemometers, 29

Army. *See* U.S. Army

Aspen, L. B., 36

Baltimore, high winds in, 56

Barnum, P. T., 63

Barnum and Bailey Circus, 6, 63

Beach, Alfred Ely, 47–48, 116

Belmont, August, 116

Bennett, Alexander, 37

Billings, Rufus, 37

Bjerknes, Vilhelm and Jacob, 123

Blizzard of 1888
  animals freeze in, 56, 57, 80
  attitudes and feelings about, 9, 30, 105–108,
    114–115
  burial of victims of, 112, **112**
  called American Storm, 100
  called Great White Hurricane, 25
  financial setbacks caused by, 105, 116
  forecasts of, 3–4, 8, 121–122
  long-term impact of, 114–117, 120–123
  and national security, 120–121
  number of casualties in, 19, 24, 112–113
  path of, 2–5, **3**, 8–9, **11**, 13–14, 16, **52**, 56,
    83, **97**, 99–100

and poor, 7, 13, **14**, **15**, 71–75, **72**, **74**,
  100–102, 105
prices raised because of, 47, 67, 100–101,
  105, 111
rain and, 3, 10, 12–16, 20
temperatures during, 14, 25, 56, 70, 103
wind speeds during, 25, 29, **34–35**, **38**, 56,
  70, 75

Blizzards, **63**, 113–114
  defined, 25
  origin of word, 25–26

Boats. *See* Transportation
  pilot, 2, 10–12, 75–78, 108–110

Bourget, Paul, 7

Brady's notion store, 37, 39–40

Brooklyn Bridge, 6–7, 49–52, **50–51**

Brubacker, William, 27–29

Campbell, Helen, 74–75

Central Park, temperature in, 56

Chadbourne, A. C., 31–33

Chapell family, 2, 54–56, 98–99

Chicago, subway built in, 116

Cleveland, Grover, 1, 120

Coal miners and mining, 105

Coal supplies, 46, 58, 73–74, 87, 101–102, **102**

Coleman, Jacob, 86–89

Colt (pilot boat), 11, 17, 75–78, 108–110

Communications. *See* Telegraph; Telephone

Conley, E. D., 110
Conkling, Roscoe, 2, 30–31, 67–70, 113
Connecticut
    Danbury, **109**
    Hartford, **122**, 124
    Montville, *See* Chapell family
    Naugatuck, **22–23**
    New Haven, 102
    South Norwalk, **90**
    Stamford, 82–83
    Waterbury, 105–108
    West Southington, **87**
Customs House, 36
Cuts, railroad, 30, 43–45, 104

Delaware River, 56
Department of Agriculture, 123
Depew, Chauncey, 41–46, 104
Depression of 1888, 36
Detroit, plowing in, 120
Dundee (Scotland), 52
Dunn, Elias, 8, 16, 29
Dunwoody, H.H.C., 13

East River, 91–96, **92–94**
Emergency plans, 117–120
Equitable Building, 5, 7, 16
Express (train), 43

Farms and farming, 2, 16, 52–56, 84, 97, 105,
    110
Firefighters, 16, 80, **81**, 84, 85, 87
"First Dandelion, The," 1
Flyer (train), 19–21, 97
Food supplies, 45–46, 52–53, 57–59, 73, 87,
    100–102, 105, 124
Friedrich, emperor of Germany, 12

Garbage and litter, 33, 115–116, 120
Garrigues, Mr., 36, 60–61
Gedney House, 33
Gomez, Manuel, 76–78
Grand Central Depot, 20, 41, 42, 43, 104
Great White Hurricane, 25

Greely, Adolphus, 121
Green, (Mr. and Mrs.) Charles, 37, 40

Hewitt, Abram, 13, 87, 115, 117
Horses
    abuse of, 47
    cost of, 47
    electrocuted by fallen wires, 59–61
    frozen, 80
    and horse-drawn vehicles, 5, 16, 27–29, **28**,
        39, **46**, 47, **58**, 80, 89, **98**, 111, **117–119**,
        124
    and milk delivery, 27–29
    pulling boatload of coal, **102**
    pulling fire engine, **81**
    pulling snowplows, **58**, 104
Housing and shelter, 6, **6**, 7, 13, **14**, 57, 71–75,
    72, 101
Hudson River, 27, 48–49, 75
Hurricanes, 14, 25, 123
Hypothermia, 24

Immigrants, 7, 43, 84
    Italian, 43–45, 71, 87, 89–90, 104, **118–119**,
        120
Inglis, William, 2, 10–12, 16–17, 75–78, 108–110
Interborough Rapid Transit Company, 116

Job security, 33–36, 88–89, 120

Knight, Spencer W., **121**

Lee, Charles, 37
Lewes (Delaware), 10, 17–19, **18**, 58, 105
Lifesaving Station, **18**, 19
Litter. *See* Garbage and litter
Long, Francis, 4–8, 16, 29–30, 31, 80

Madison Square Garden, 63
Maher, Patrick, 111
Mail, 46, 58, 104, **121**
Marshall, James, 2, 37, 66, 97–98, 110
Marshall, John H., 2, 10, 17–19, 57–59, 103
Mary Heitman (boat), 49

Massachusetts
  Boston, 27, 31, 43, 103, 116
    Northampton, **88**
Meisinger, John J., 2, 12, 63–64
Milk deliveries, 27–29, 45–46, 73, 100, 124
Missions, 74
Mitchell, Charlie, 12
Morgue, storm victims in, **112**
Morrow, May, 2, 36, 59–65

National Disaster Survey Report, 114
National Weather Service, 3, 121, 124
Newark Bay, 37
New Haven Railroad, 31
New Jersey
  Elizabeth, 36–37, 65–66, 97
  Hoboken, 75
  Jersey City, 27
  Newark, 116, **118–119**
  Princeton, 19
Newspapers, 2, 78–79, 80–83, 105–108. *See also* Inglis; Reilly
  Albany *Journal,* 27
  Albany *Times,* 82–83
  Bellows Falls *Times,* 83
  Hartford *Courant,* 124
  New York *Eagle,* 111–112
  New York *Herald,* 1, 12
  New York *Morning* Journal, **78–79**
  New York *Sun,* 41, 45, 82, 95–96, 105
  New York Times, 115, 124
  New York Tribune, 47
  New York *World,* 11, 110
  Providence *Journal,* 59
New York (State)
  Albany, 20–21, 27, 82, 97, 108
  Bronx, 14–15
  Brooklyn, 2, 8, **26**, 37, 48, 91–96, **92–94, 102**
  Buffalo, 2, 19–20, 27, 97
  Coney Island, 111
  Liberty, 56
  Long Island, 2, 16, 48, 54, 97, 100, 123
  Poughkeepsie, 105

Staten Island, 37, 48–49, 66, 110
New York Central Railroad, 41–46
New York City, **4, 5,** 5–7, 12, **26, 28, 34–35, 42, 44,** 46, **60–61, 68–69, 117.** *See also* Chadbourne; Conkling; Morrow; Strong; *and specific topics*
  antilitter laws in, 33, 116
  cost of blizzard to businesses in, 116
  department stores in, 63
  entertainment, restaurants, and saloons in, 5–6, 13, 62–64, **63, 65,** 75, 100
  and frozen East River, 91–96, **92–94**
  as "ghost town," 80
  isolated by blizzard, 52
  long-term impact of blizzard on, 114–120
  politics of, 48, **100,** 115–117
  poor in, **7,** 13, **14, 15,** 71–75, **72, 74,** 100–102, 105
  Sabbath laws in, 13
  traffic congestion in, 47
  warm winter of 1888 in, 1, 103
  wealthy citizens of, 6, **6, 15,** 45
New York City Hotel, 56
New York Club, 70, 113
New York Harbor, 10–12
New-York Historical Society, 114

Old London Building, 56

Philadelphia, 14, 26, 47, 56, 82, 103, 116
Poles. *See* Wires and poles
Police, 16, 49–52, 75, 80, 84, 85, 87, 92, 101
Protector (tugboat), 17–18

Randall, Sam, 2, 16, 54, 97
Reilly, Richard C., 2, 111–112
Ridley and Sons department store, 2, 63–64
Russell, Charles Edward, 72–73

Schools and schoolchildren, 27, 37–40, 53
Scientific American, 47
Scientific American Building, **46**
S. E. Babcock (tugboat), 96
Shelter. *See* Housing and shelter

Ships. *See* Transportation: Boats and ships

Signal Corps, 3, 8, 12–13, 121–123

Singer Sewing Machine factory, 36–37, 65–66, 97

Snow removal, 2, 12, **22–23**, **42**, 42–46, **58**, 84–90, **86–88**, **87**, **90**, 100, **100**, 103–104, **106–107**, 108, **109**, 116–120, **118–119**

    and deaths, 113

    and politicians, **100**, 116–120

    wages paid for, 43, 89

Snow shovels, 2, 12, 63–64. *See also* Snow removal

Society of Blizzard Men and Blizzard Ladies of 1888, 114, **126–127**

Stark, Otto, **68–69**

Steidler, George, 73–74

Storms, 14, 25, **63**, 113–114, 123–124. *See also* Blizzard of 1888

Streetlights, 5, 61

Strong, Sam, 37–40

Sullivan, John L., 12

Sulzer, William, 67

Superstorm of 1993, 114

Tamesei (steamship), 17

Telegraph, 3, 16, 27, 36, 41, 59–61, 80, 84, 98, 115, 121, 124

Telephones, 7, 55, 59–61, 84, 98, 121

Tenements, 72–74

Transportation, 16, **44**, **46**, 46–52, **50–51**, 115

    boats and ships, 2, 10–12, 16–19, **18**, 49, 75–78, **77**, **94**, 94–96, **102**, 103, 108–110, **111**, 112

    ferries, 27, 48–49, 84–85

    rowboats, 37, 66

    sleighs, 47, 89, **98**, 111

    streetcars and cable cars, 15–16, 39, **46**, 47–49, **58**, **117**, 124

    trains, 19–21, **22–23**, **30**, **31–32**, 32, 41–46, **42**, 49, 57–59, 84, 97, 103–105, **104**, 124

    trains, elevated, 14, 15, 36, 46, 78, **79**

    trains, milk, 27, 46, 105

    trains, subway, 47–48, 116

Tweed, William Marcy ("Boss"), 48

Twombly, Harrison, 45

U.S. Army, 3, 30, 122. *See also* Signal Corps

U.S. Department of Agriculture, 123

U.S. National Weather Service, 3, 121, 124

U.S. Weather Bureau, 123

Vanderbilt, William H., 41–42, 45

Van Wyck, Frederick, 45

Vermont

    Bellows Falls, 83

    Brattleboro, **98**, **121**

    newspaper coverage of blizzard in, 83, 105

    Northfield, 56

    schoolchildren led home in, 53

Virginia

    Norfolk, heavy rain in, 14

    Tidewater, flood in, 53

Washington, D.C., 1, 120–121, 124

    as weather forecasting headquarters, 3, 8, 29

Weather Bureau, 123

Weather forecasts, 3–4, 8, 112–113, 121–124. *See also* Weather stations

    modern, 123–124

Weather indications, 3. *See also* Weather forecasts

Weather Proverbs, 13

Weather stations, 3, 8, 12–13, 29, 121

    New York City, 4–5, 8, 16, 29–30, 80

Weinstein, Irving, 78–80

Whiskey, 28, 40, 64, 65, **74**, **99**

Whitman, Walt, 1

Wilhelm I of Germany, 12

Wilson, P. M., 101–102

Wilson, Sara, 2, 19–24, 97

Wires and poles, **34–35**, 59–61, **60–61**, 80, 84, 115, 120–121

Women

    and job security, 36

    and social customs, 62, 64

Work and workers, 16, 27–37, 56, 84, **86**, 105, 116–120

    Italian laborers, **42**, 43–45, 71, 87, 89–90, 104, **118–119**, 120

working poor, 71, 100